Salvation: It's Not What I Thought It Was

Salvation: It's Not What I Thought It Was

Don R. Vining

WINEPRESS WP PUBLISHING

© 1999 by Don R. Vining. All rights reserved

Printed in the United States of America

Packaged by WinePress Publishing, PO Box 428, Enumclaw, WA 98022.

No part of this publication may be reproduced, stored in a retrieval system, or transmitted in any way by any means—electronic, mechanical, photocopy, recording, or otherwise—without the prior permission of the copyright holder, except as provided by USA copyright law.

Unless otherwise noted all scriptures are taken from the King James Version of the Holy Bible.

ISBN 1-57921-177-1
Library of Congress Catalog Card Number: 99-63465

"This is a good book, especially for all young pastors who are establishing and growing a church. Don Vining is one of our most dedicated young pastors in the Church of God."

> Larry J. Timmerman
> Church of God
> General Evangelism & Home Missions Department

"Pastor Vining has captured and brought into focus the fundamental position we all need to stand...in Christ. This message will ignite a fire under, and confront, the lukewarm and zealous alike. It flows into the reader's life like a river—and results in an alignment with the presence of Christ."

> Dr. Carol Bartholomew
> Chiropractic Physician
> Ocala, FL

"Highly readable. Rev. Vining's book is valuable—and sometimes entertaining—in its insistence that there is no other way but to simply accept Jesus and live the higher life in Him. He speaks with freshness and originality."

> Tom Frye, Ph.D.
> Clinical Director
> Heart of Florida Boy's Ranch

"A must read for *non*-converts, *new* converts and *seasoned* converts. It is not a biased conservative view but a fresh view in layman's terminology."

> Willis Canada
> Gospel Recording Artist
> Richmond, VA

"In an age of pat answers and mixed messages, this book speaks clearly and directly about what true Christianity involves. Must reading for anyone who has wondered if Christianity is about more than walking a church aisle."

> Robert D. Smith
> Co-Founder & President
> Andrews & Associates, Inc.
> Franklin, TN

This book is dedicated to my wonderful wife, Kay, without whose love and unconditional support there would be a great void in my ministry. Also to my two loving daughters, Sheena—who has a heart full of compassion—and Brittany—who has the kind of faith that can kill a Goliath.

Acknowledgments

My thanks to Dr. Tom Frye for his direction and encouragement, Pastor Nate for speaking God's Word into my spirit concerning this project, Dr. Carol Bartholomew for her prayerful insight, and Robert Smith for his council in publishing.

Thanks also to my ever-loving parents, whom I can depend upon to be with me when battles come—Dad standing by my side and Mother in her prayer closet.

My appreciation to Connie Neumann, who only by God's anointing could have taken five hundred pages of material and captured my personality and message in this book.

A special thank you to the people of the Intensive Care Ministries for allowing me to be their shepherd and to lead them into a greater understanding of God's Holy Word.

Contents

CHAPTER ONE: GIVERS, TAKERS & JERKS **17**
   In Versus *Of* or *With* 18
   Unchanged Christians 18
   The Three Kinds of People 20
   Coattail Christians 23
   Take Time to Learn 25
   What Kind of Christian Are You? 26

CHAPTER TWO: LESSONS FROM THE FIRE **29**
   Just Stop it! 30
   Sudden Loss/Long-term Gain 31
   Whom Do You Serve? 36

CHAPTER THREE: FEEDING THE HUNGER **39**
   God-based Living 41
   Growth Takes Time 43

Our Position in Christ 45
　　Give Yourself a Check-up 47

CHAPTER FOUR: IT ALL STARTS WITH BIRTH **51**
　　Out with the Old 52
　　True Christians are Givers 54
　　Starting Over 54
　　The New Birth 56

CHAPTER FIVE: INTIMATE CHANGE **61**
　　Know the Word 62
　　No Band-Aids 64
　　What Are You Doing? 65

CHAPTER SIX: GROWING IN GRACE **71**
　　Growth Takes Time 72
　　Growth is Essential 73
　　Grace Produces Devotion 73
　　Too Much Too Soon 74
　　Prepare the Soil 75
　　Process, not Product 77

CHAPTER SEVEN: MEEKNESS IS NOT WEAKNESS **81**
　　Something is Brewing 82
　　Changing Tracks 83
　　Elements of Grace 85
　　The Value of Virtue 85
　　Faith Follows 87
　　The Meaning of *Meekness* 88

Chapter Eight: Stand Firm **91**
    Gentleness, not Judgment 92
    Examples to Follow 93
    Stand for Your Faith 96

Chapter Nine: Smile—and Shut Up **101**
    Know What Came Before—and What's Ahead 102
    Rejoice Anyway 106
    Seek Self-control 109
    Trust and Obey 110
    Peace in the Storm 112

Chapter Ten: Rejoice in Hope **115**
    Running Ahead of God 116
    Patience in Tribulation 117
    Keep Hope Alive 120
    Patience—Right Now 123

Chapter Eleven: Instant Prayer **127**
    Change Hurts 128
    Prime the Pump 129
    "Now I Lay Me Down to Sleep...." 132
    Never Quit 133

Chapter Twelve: The Spirit of Forgiveness **137**
    But You Promised 140
    Forgiveness Demands Action 142

Chapter Thirteen: Sin's Payment **145**
    The Willing Substitute 147
    Connected Threads 148

The Perfect Lamb 149
Demands of Grace 150
How Many Times? 153

Chapter Fourteen: The Radiant Life 155
Useful Servants 157
Inward Change/Outward Evidence 159
Make Your Choice 161
Radiance Shines 162
Do You Want a Personal Relationship
   with Jesus Christ? 165

Bibliography 167

Chapter One

Givers, Takers, and Jerks

After years of serving the Lord, I'm finding out being a Christian is different from everything I've been taught. To say *I've accepted Christ* is nothing more than saying *I've made a decision to turn my life around*. But that is not the end of the story; it is the beginning. I've found it takes a long time to become a *Christian*, which literally means "little Christ." So you don't think I am just babbling, I'm going to prove it to you. In 2 Corinthians it says, "Therefore if any man be in Christ"—not *of Christ*, not *for Christ*, but *in Christ*—"he is a new creature: old things are passed away, behold…" (5:17). What does *behold* mean? It means to hush up and listen. It means to tune in and pay attention because God's about to reveal something He said. Behold, He says, all things—not some of the things, not part of the things, not the things you choose—but "all things are become new." Everything.

In Versus *Of* or *With*

Like it or not, every person is *in* something. You're either *in*secure, *in*volved, *in*terrupted, or *in*sane; but you're *in* something because we're all involved in this thing called *life*, in this place called a *world*. We're all in to something. Paul said if any man be in Christ, something is different. Something's going to change; something's not going to be like it was yesterday. I'm not going to show up the same as I did last night, because this morning I am in Christ. You won't catch me watching what I've always watched on television, because now I'm in something. I'm not in the world; I'm not into Satanism; I'm not into Buddhism; I'm not into something phony; I'm *in* Christ.

We come to Christ in faith, and Christ comes to us in power. He saved me from a life of sin, but where's the power? That's what I want to ask each of you: Where's the power? I'm going to blow away your concept of what a Christian is and mess up your way of thinking. Being a Christian is more than what I ever believed it to be and more than I ever received.

I've always said, "Praise God I'm saved, so I'm a new creature." But how can I be a new creature if I haven't left old things? If I haven't changed my ways or changed my thinking or changed the way I dress? If I haven't changed the way I act, the people I hang out with, or the things I say? How can I be in Christ when the old things are just as alive as they've always been?

Unchanged Christians

I have seen too many unchanged Christians. Often people in the Church spend so much time shouting when someone makes a decision for Christ that they never take time out to say, "By the way, partner, now that you've made a decision there's a lot of hard work ahead of you because now you have to become a Christian. Now you have to change your thinking. You have to change the way you hang out and where you hang out, and you have to change your friends. Now you're also going to have to start spending your money differently." We don't take time to share that. Why? Because, praise God, if we get them saved and have them crying and in that mode of feeling, we're afraid if we put the burden of change on them, they're going to leave. We live in fear that we're going to lose them…when we're losing anyway.

If it's really God and it's really love, you'll set them free, and they will return to you. The more we hold on, the more we lose. For instance, if I take my spouse—so precious and kind and loving—and put her in a box of jealousy and treat her as if I can't trust her to go to the restroom on her own, soon enough I'll lose her. But if it's really God and I really trust the love, I will set her free, and if she's gone for a day or two, or if she's gone to the mall or the grocery store, I'll know she is coming back home. We hold on thinking we're saving, nourishing, cherishing, and all the time we're losing.

The kind of change I'm talking about is when the characteristics of a person change. You see, salvation—receiving Christ—is one level. The characteristics and the character of the person changing are an entirely different level. That's a different ball game, a new story, a brand new chapter. Do you ever get tired of just reading and reliving chapter one? I've been in chapter one so long it's sickening. I want to open chapter two for you. It's a joy to be saved and it's wonderful to feel, feel, feel Christ come into my life. It's a wonderful feeling. But somehow that feeling must be turned into faith or it will never last. Have you been saved at least a couple of hundred times? That is because we don't understand true salvation.

We say, "He's saved me and I'm happy within myself, so I don't have to worry about the world or even the salvation of my neighbor." We hold on to what we have, but all the time we're losing it because we're holding on so tightly.

You lose your miracle if you hold on to it. You've got to set free what God has given you and see what He'll do with it. Take that miracle and say, "Go in Jesus name." If hoarding and selfishness and self-centeredness are in your heart, that is what you are going to speak and what is going to be the evidence of your stand for Christ.

The Three Kinds of People

I have found there are three kinds of people. I've been able to categorize myself, too, so let me put it this way. There are times in my life when I'm a taker. *Gimme, gimme, gimme, gimme, gimme.* Then there are times in my life when I'm just a flat-out jerk. And then there are times in my life when I'm a giver, a true child of God, because I've got to give somebody what I've got and let somebody see what He's worked in my life. You see, there are takers and jerks, and then there are givers. There are believers, true believers, who would say, "God, why would you save me when there is someone else who could be saved? Why would you touch me with a miracle when someone else needed that miracle?"

A young man left one of our services crying. When asked what was wrong, he said he was out of work and didn't have enough money to buy his mother a Christmas gift. When I gave him fifty dollars, he cried even harder and said, "You should have given that money to someone who needed it more." Humility is saying, "God, I don't deserve this." If you are really in Christ, you sit and weep and say, "Lord, I don't deserve what you have given me." He will say to you, "Oh, because I love you, I've given."

I am determined to change people's ways of thinking. What are the characteristics of a true believer? Once you've made a decision to follow Christ, this next change, the character change, has to take place. It's more intense, more involved, more direct, and more than a matter of fact.

There were times I went home upset with my pastor because he preached right at me. I approached him later and asked, "Why did you preach at me and make a spectacle out of this?" He said, "I didn't even know you were there Sunday!"

In Hebrews 4:12 we find that sometimes the Word comes "piercing even to the dividing asunder of soul and spirit, and of the joints and marrow, and is a discerner of the thoughts and intents of the heart." It sets you apart and messes you up. It's not a man; it's the Word. By His spirit He comes to replace that worldly character with a godly character. He can't put something in until He takes something out. And He can't take something out until He rips something up. When you are writing a report and you mess up the paper, what do you do? You rip it out and start all over again. That's what He has to do. We have to say, "God rip some pages out of this book. There are a few chapters I'm not real pleased with, and I know if I'm not pleased, you can't be pleased."

"If any man be in Christ," he's no longer in himself. He's no longer one of the characters that says *me, me, me, my, my, my, gimme, gimme, gimme*. He's not a jerk. I don't want you to be offended, but I pray that you will ask the spirit of the Lord to show you when you are a taker and when you are a jerk, and ask Him to protect you from those times. "Lord, let somebody see Christ in my life." If you appear as Christ today, then you are a jerk tomorrow, you are going to mess up somebody's comprehension of what the true Christ is all about because Christ is not a jerk. He said that if any man be in Christ, he is a new creature. Something's different; something's changed; something's permanent. You don't sew a patch on and then cut it off in the morning. You don't intentionally wear a shirt today that says, "I'm a taker" and tomorrow wear a shirt that says, "I'm a jerk" and the next day one that reads, "I'm a child of God."

How can anyone know what we believe in if that's how we live? The character of the Christian has to change. The mentality has to change so that when we are lost in ourselves, we find ourselves in Christ. Just as blood refurbishes the body, His spirit refurbishes the godly spirit that was in a person. He renews, refreshes, changes, cleanses, and makes different. His blood can flow through you this day and change you. He can mess up your way of thinking and can make you see something you haven't seen before. He can cause you to get in His Word, and He can show you what it means. I wish every one of you would go and buy a set of commentaries. Instead of studying a whole book of the Bible, just take that one verse and say, "God teach me what you are saying." Often, what we see on the surface is not what He means in the spirit. That is why it says, "Study to show thyself approved," in 2 Timothy 2:15.

In the phrase "If any man be in Christ," *in* means "surrounded or contained by, subject to, inside." If any man be in Christ, he can't be in the house with all the doors and windows open. It means "surrounded by Christ." The Bible didn't say if any man be *of* Christ. There are a lot of "of" personalities out there. I see children dressed like rock stars, professional sports stars, or popular people. When Michael Jackson was so popular, I saw kids running around wearing one glove. It was a fad, just like some of the new words kids say.

Recently, one of my nieces looked at me and said, "You are phat." Well, bump you. She said, "No, you don't understand. *P-h-a-t* means 'cool.'" So now I guess I can walk up to somebody and say, "Man, you are phat." I can go to a camp meeting and say, "I've got the phatest bunch of people you've ever seen." Our minds are so goofed up that we say we're one thing, but we live something else. Just like trying to understand slang, we have to dig into the Bible and see if that's what it really means.

It is one thing to be *with* Christ, but it is another to be *in* Him. If we had walked the streets of Capernaum and Jerusalem with

Jesus, we probably wouldn't have thought much about it. Just another day with Christ; it's just Jesus. The Bible says a man named Nicodemus had a long conversation with Christ, but it doesn't appear he ever returned for another. Think about it. Judas was with Christ throughout His ministry, yet He betrayed Him. In one sense we've been with Christ, because we've been raised that there is a God and that there is a Jesus. We've been raised to believe there is a Holy Spirit and a Bible. We have heard all of those things. But to hear about those things doesn't necessarily make you in sympathy or in union with the person of Christ. It just means you know who He is. Just like knowing who is your pastor is different from being in the pastor and sharing his vision.

Coattail Christians

Something has happened to me because I am in Christ. The new creature comes out. It's not enough to hold on to the coattail of Christ. It is not enough to live my life speaking well of Christ. In Matthew 7:21–23, Jesus had this to say:

> Not everyone that saith unto me, Lord, Lord, shall enter into the kingdom of heaven; but he that doeth the will of my Father which is in heaven. Many will say to me in that day, Lord, Lord, have we not prophesied in thy name? and in thy name have cast out devils? and in thy name done many wonderful works? And then I will profess unto them, I never knew you: depart from me, ye that work iniquity.

It is not enough to say I'm a worker for Christ. It is not enough to say I know Christ died on the cross. There has to be a change on the inside. An orange looks really nice on the outside, but until you get into that thing, you don't really know how good it is.

I have done business with people who could quote Scripture. I once signed a contract, and while I was signing it, the man was quoting "And we know that all things work together for good to them that love God" (Rom. 8:28a). That man was taking advantage of God's people while quoting Scripture, and I knew it. When I walked away I had to say, "Jerk." I'm not going to be fooled by a false face and neither should you. God certainly isn't fooled. Sometimes you have to ask Christ, "Is this person a taker, a giver, or a jerk?" But you can't ask for that wisdom and knowledge until after you realize there is something wrong with you.

I thought I was a believer. I had been living off the passion and the feeling that He saved me from a life of sin. I thought that was all there was to it. But it isn't; it is just the beginning. Shame on you if you've been saved for a year and don't have some favorite scriptures by now. When you are in Christ, you want to know more about Him. I was married to my wife for several years before I really began to get into her heart and recognize that she was more than a person there to meet my needs. As I began to see her characteristics, I was shocked because she was a stranger to me. She was so pure in her thoughts and motives that I wondered if she had tripped out on something. As I got into her heart I began to see how big a role she was to play in my vision. She got into me and began to see that I wasn't always a jerk. Something intimate was happening to our spirits. Two were becoming one. You can't become as one until you get to know that person. Husbands and wives, sons and daughters, and brothers and sisters live together for years, totally ignorant of the feelings and the heart of the ones they live beside.

It is often the same way in our relationship to Christ. We get so wrapped up in what we *think* a Christian should be, that we don't get in the book and find out what a Christian really *is*. The enemy wants you to be a casual drinker at the fountain of life. He knows you won't be nearly as effective then as you would be if you got into the water and stayed under the spout where the power is coming out. He knows if he can make you believe that "just a dab will do you," then you'll never cause him any harm. It's one thing to be two people living side by side. It's another thing to be in that person, finding out what is in their heart. It's one thing to be of Christ; it's another to be in Christ. Are you a taker, a jerk, or a child of God? What is your passion? Not every person that says *Lord, Lord* will enter into the kingdom.

If any man be in Christ, he must love Him. To love Him means more than blind affectionate instincts or clinging attachments or sudden emotions. That's not love. Love is when you love someone no matter how they look in the morning. Love makes you look up and believe in something you've never believed in. Love gets you out of the natural and puts you into the supernatural. I've never received a miracle except by faith believing I could receive a miracle. If any man be in Christ, He loves Christ. He does more than hold on to the coattail of Christ. If any man be in Christ, the selfishness is going to go. There are lots of folks who know a lot about Christ, but they have never entered into Christ at all. To have the mind of Christ is to be able to think as He does, to love as He loves, and to receive as He receives. If any man be in Christ, there is something different and it tells.

Take Time to Learn

Paul was on the road to Damascus going to tear apart Christianity, when He had an encounter with Christ. Acts 9 tells us he made a decision right then and there and said, "I'm going to serve you." Sometimes when we're hurting—and some of us don't even know we are hurting— Christ comes to us and says, "I want to touch you." Sometimes He reaches out to you before you get to reach out to Him. Paul made an immediate decision, but he didn't start his ministry until almost three years later. Do you know what he did during that time? When Christ touched his life, even as educated as he was, Paul set himself apart to learn what the Father would have him know. We can learn a lot from Paul.

Too many people come into the Church, get saved, and then get mad at the preacher if he doesn't put them right into a ministry position. In one three-week period, every single young believer I had put into a ministry position resigned, quit, or left a nasty letter sitting on my desk. It was my fault. The Word warns us about putting those with childlike faith into ministry positions. When Paul came out of his time of "training, discipling, learning, and hearing from the Father," his message was so powerful that the religious leaders immediately wanted to kill Him (Acts 9:23–24). This guy had a word from God. Initially, Paul knew enough about Christ to persecute Him, but after his encounter with Christ, he said, "I'm going to take a couple of years and let God teach me some things." After that, no one had to question if he was a man of God.

Just because I know of Christ doesn't put me in sympathy or union with Him. That happens only when I get into Him and let Him teach me. Look at the emphasis Paul put on the word *in*. It is to be in Christ that makes one a new creature. In Philippians 3:9 he said, "My wish is to be found in Him." Not of Him, not by Him, not through Him, but *in* Him.

What Kind of Christian Are You?

As I put this material together, I found myself sobbing because what I thought a Christian was, is not a Christian. I was living that He was Christ and that He had made a difference in my life, but I never really knew the mind of the One who saved me. *What* was on His mind when He gave His life? What was on His mind when

He said "my grace is sufficient"? What's on His mind for you? What is on His mind with that miracle? Why did He save you and heal you? So you can be a taker or a jerk, or so you can give? Christ is a giver. He'll go to the scum of the earth and He'll bring love. He'll feed you and dress you with the shirt off His back. He said, in essence, "Come and drink of this water, and I'll show you something you have never found before."

There is a world of difference between being of Christ and being in Christ. Are you a giver, a taker, or a jerk? If we are truly in Christ, the world's going to see something in us they've never seen before.

Chapter Two

Lessons from the Fire

Every day should be a new beginning in some area of your life. There should be something you learn about yourself spiritually, so you can say, "I am not going to be like this tomorrow." If the world can't see Christ in our lives—for we are the light of the world—then what good is the Church? What good are we to the world? For too long we have asked the world, "What can you offer us?" It is time for the Church to say to the world, "Here is what He can give you. He's given us salvation and peace of mind. He has allowed us to walk through the valley of the shadow of death, only to find He was there. He's allowed us to visit the mountaintop, only to see that by His mighty hand, He was there. He's allowed us to walk through the balanced places of life, to see that He was there, too. Whatever you are facing this moment—good or bad—God is there for you." One day the devil is going to tell you you're a worthless, useless piece of garbage, and you're not going to make it. When that happens, remember this: God has something for you. You are His creation, and you are worth something.

In the summer of 1998, I watched the fires burning here in Florida. I believe there was a message tied to those fires. We saw the country reach out to us with the finest firefighters and equipment, but I believe God was saying, "No matter how much you love and care for one another, you'll not conquer this battle without me." We are living in the last days, and I don't believe we will have many more opportunities to sit in the presence of the Lord and decide if we will follow Christ or deny Him.

Just Stop It!

It is time for America to stop. It's time for believers to stop. It's time for us to quit leaning on what we learned in the last twenty, thirty, forty, or fifty years and just stop. After your child questions you forty or fifty times about something, do you ever look at them and say, "JUST STOP IT!"? I believe God is telling believers, "STOP IT!"

One day a man rolled his car right through a stop sign. A police officer saw him and stopped him. He said to the man, "You ran right through that stop sign."

The man responded, "But officer, I slowed down."

The officer took out his nightstick and began to beat the man on the head. *Wop, wop, wop.* "Now," he said, "do you want me to slow down, or do you want me to stop?"

I believe with all my heart that God wants His people to stop and take a look at what they really believe. We must take a look at this so-called religion we've grabbed hold of.

During the fires, every newspaper showed scorched earth on the front page. We saw homes that had been destroyed and people without hope. We can compare what happened here in Florida to the storms and clouds of our lives. Sometimes we don't know which way to run to get out of the fire. The clouds are so thick, we don't know if we should go north, south, east, or west. We're baffled and confused until we're not even sure there is a God because our world is falling apart. Even the world says, "Pray for us." But they know not what they say. Our God is not a Band-Aid God. He is not going to stop the flames and torching moments of our lives and then have us turn around and make a mockery of His Word.

A time is coming when God's people will have to get into the spirit, walk in the spirit, and stay in the spirit—or they will find destruction. Through these pictures, I feel God was saying, "Son, even though many folks look good on the outside, they're scorched, burned, and smoked out on the inside. There's so much silent frustration in them that they don't know where to turn. In the midnight hour, the devil plays with their minds."

In the midst of the storm, too many people pray their petty-minded prayers, and when they shed a tear and find peace for a moment, they fool themselves into believing that because God came on the scene, that's it. They don't need God any longer—until the next trial. I believe God is shaking His Church and His people. The Bible says if any man be in Christ, old things are passed away; behold all things become new.

Sudden Loss/Long-term Gain

You have to have a sudden loss to have a long-term gain. Something has to be lost, and it must be an immediate loss. We need to say, "Lord, I'm tired of believing in myself. I need to be in you, not just holding on to you. I need more than just a meal or a Band-Aid. I need more than a bulldozer to plow around my fire or a tanker to sprinkle me down, cool me off, and make me feel better. Lord, I need something that will go to the innermost being and lift me up. I want people to see the changes and know that I've been to Calvary."

You can't say you're in Christ and yet continue to sin. You can't say God has saved you, changed you, and turned your life around, if you are still addicted to the things of the world. God is not a part-time God. God doesn't come and heal half of leukemia; He comes in and He heals all of it. He doesn't come in and heal half of a nervous condition; He heals all of it. God is a sovereign God! When He comes in, people listen. People take notice, even when they don't want to acknowledge He's in the house.

Someone came to me recently and told me about a brother in Christ who was going through a tough time. It didn't make sense to me; I thought that person was doing well. As I thought about it, the spirit of the Lord said, *"The voice that said, 'I'm struggling' is the devil that has been trying to destroy that person. The devil is saying there's been more of God in that individual recently, and he's having a hard time conquering what Almighty God is doing."*

God is not slack concerning His Word (2 Pet. 3:9). Once you enter into Him by faith, He enters into you by power. Once that power comes, an anointing comes so that no matter what you speak out of your lips, He's still God on the inside. He's still the God that stands. There are times we are crippled in areas of our lives, and the devil screams out, "That bunch is teaching everyone how to know the wiles and the temptations of the enemy, and we're having a hard time conquering!"

I believe God is showing believers all across this country that if the devil's fighting you, it means you are targeted for a miracle. God has set you up for a spectacular moment. He's planning a party and somebody's about to light your candle! That should get us excited. That should make us say, "God let my candles burn.

Let there be a party in my life. God, I'm tired of fear and anxiety and worry. I'm tired of saying I'm a child of God, but I'm depressed all the time." If any man be in Christ, then Christ is in him. If any man be in Christ, old things stand no more. That means we can't go to church and proclaim we've been bought by the blood and then go home and have to take a little drink. That means we can't say God delivered us from the filth of the world, but we can't wait to watch "As the Stomach Turns." We want spirit-filled homes; we want God to do the miraculous; we want the supernatural to come, but we're still holding on to Him instead of getting in Him.

We've talked about the three different types of people who call themselves believers: givers, takers, and jerks. Those who know just enough about the Word, and how to—I call it "whodo"—someone, are jerks. They get what they want and then drag you out in the middle of the desert and leave you there for the buzzards to eat your carcass. John 10:10 says the enemy comes to steal, kill, and destroy. It never said my brothers in the Lord come to steal and kill and destroy. That tells me anyone who comes to tear apart must be of the devil, and not of the most high God. Oh, be careful who you let in your home. Be careful who your children run around with. Be careful about what they watch on the tube. If any man be in Christ, he's a new creature. He's brand new. He's fresh. He's different. There's a glow about him that make-up can't give him. You can wash make-up off, but real change sticks.

If any man be in Christ; if any church be in Christ; if any people be in Christ, then Christ has to be in them by power. I have heard people say they like being Pentecostal, but they don't like a bunch of hoopla. I heard one preacher say, "Why am I yelling? Because I'll explode if I don't." When God comes alive in you, then you've got something that's got to come out. You need to tell someone about Jesus. In Revelation 3:20, Jesus Christ said, "Behold I stand at the door and knock." I'm hoping you'll open up for me and let me in. I'm hoping you'll give me that opportunity. I'm hoping you'll get into me and let me get into you. I'm hoping someone will be in Christ.

We don't have another hundred years to decide if we are going to serve God. We don't have another ten years for our children to be under our roofs to see Christ in our lives and in our homes. We don't have much time left. He said the time is now. In Matthew 10:7 He said to preach that the kingdom of God is at hand. First Corinthians 15:52 reminds us that at any moment, in the twinkling of an eye, we could be out of here, but only, only, only those that are in Christ. Remember that Christ said not all who say "Lord, Lord" will enter into the kingdom.

I have been saying, "Lord, I'm cleaning up my act and being all I can be, and you are showing me things, but I'm walking through the valley. At times fear comes, and I'm confused and sometimes I don't understand." It's a wonderful moment when you can get into the spirit and recognize it as the spirit. If you're not careful, that feeling comes across as fear. It can feel like your blood is boiling on the inside. You think something's wrong. You are living right, but the devil's trying to take you out.

When we get into Scripture, we need to look beneath the surface and dig into it. We need to ask, "Lord, what meaneth this?" It would do some of you good to start asking questions before you just buy into stuff—hook, line, and sinker. When I asked the Lord what it means to be in Christ, He said, *"I'm glad you asked. I'm going to show you."* He showed me you can't put on a new suit of clothes and have the old one underneath it. You can't put a new sock on one foot and a smelly sock on the other. You can't walk in and say, "Lord, Lord" on Sunday and then go out and live like the world on Monday. You can't be either/or. The Bible talks plainly about those who are lukewarm in Revelation 3:16. In fact, God deals rather harshly with folks who are lukewarm. He said essentially, "I wish you would let me know if you are going to be a rank sinner. It would be better if you decide to get out and stay out than for you to play games with me."

In the early '90s, Joyce Meyers, a wonderful teacher, gave a prophetic word that in the late '90s there would come a great shaking in the body of Christ. We are seeing a great shaking. God is finding out once and for all who His people are and who they aren't. You can no longer run around and say you are in Christ but still hold on to the old things.

If He's God enough to save you, then He's God enough to deliver you from the days of old and the things of old. The Bible says all things become new. Your attitude becomes new. Your concept is new. The way you spend your money is new. The way you treat your children is new.

If we want revival to come and God to genuinely come in and change our lives and our children's lives, then we have to ask Him to make us what He wants us to be. Many children struggle because we want them saved unto mom and dad or unto brother and sister. We want them saved the way we want them saved and then, after they are saved, if they don't do the things we think they should do, we put so much pressure on them that they run from God.

The only way I can coerce you into accepting Christ is to love you into Christ. A young lady got up to sing a special one Sunday morning. God was really moving in her life and the whole church was touched and blessed because we had seen God intimately changing her life. Then another morning she stood up to sing with the meanest look on her face. Her attitude said, "If you want what I've got, then pay the price like I did." You see, she suddenly thought she was something special and that destroyed her whole testimony.

We are nothing except for Jesus Christ. When God comes on me in an intimate way, it makes me want to love you. It makes me want to overlook your weakness and reach out and say, "I care for you." He saved us from a life of sin and if by true repentance we get into Him by faith, He will definitely come into us by power. But is there any evidence in your life that God is in you? You say you shout and speak in tongues. The devil speaks in tongues too. You say you witness. So does the devil. He promised Jesus a whole stinking city. We don't have anything that the devil doesn't have, except when we get in Christ and He gets in us. Then, we start to recognize when the devil comes against us. When the devil wants to mess you up, God will show you you're about to mess him up.

Why are things changing? Why is God moving in a special way? Because there are folks getting in Christ. There are people who are tired of worshipping on the surface. The world needs to see us coming in as believers and going out as believers. The world doesn't need to see us coming in as a believer on Sunday and hanging out at the bar on Monday. The world doesn't need that. The world needs to see something that is pure and holy.

Whom Do You Serve?

Is what I have in my life just an image of Christ someone has taught me? Is that what is in my life, or is there a feeling that in a supernatural way God is beginning to take control of my life? Is the God you have in you the God somebody told you about or the God you learned about by experience? I don't like anybody trying to tell me how to drive a tractor because I'm experienced, and I know what I'm doing on a tractor. But some of us are claiming to know things we really don't know. We're wearing the name and the face, but on the inside it is the same old stuff. Is the Christ in you based on what somebody told you about Christ? Or is the Christ in you because of an experience? He touched you and picked you up?

If any man, church, or ministry be in Christ, the old ways of thinking, the old attitudes, old purposes, old reasons for giving, and old things are gone, gone, gone. We're not going to live like we did yesterday. We're not going to act like we acted yesterday and not going to say the things we said yesterday. I'm not going to be the person next Sunday that I was last Sunday. I'm going to be something different because I found something new in the Word this week—not last week, last month, or last year—but this week. He's taken old things and He's kicking them out.

That means something is coming on me that's never been on me before. It's not coming from my mind but from my heart. Do you ever say, "Why did I think that? Where did that come from?" The Holy Spirit says that came from deep within. "Greater is he that is in you, than he that is in the world" (1 John 4:4). When you get in Christ and old things go away, you stop living in fear. You start living in peace and joy and happiness. Your desire becomes, "God I want more of you; God teach me."

I feel compelled to say to each and every one of you, STOP. Stop what you're doing. Don't roll through this stop sign. Stop. Some of you have been buffaloed into praying a prayer. You've been told that if you pray the sinner's prayer, you'll be saved and everything will be OK. But when you get home, you don't feel anything, and you wonder if you've been saved at all. You didn't feel anything then, and you don't feel anything now. Understand that the sinner's prayer simply means you have made a decision to turn your life around. Salvation starts off real small. It starts as a decision. Then as you pursue God, you will find that the light begins to seep through the cracks and the crannies of your life.

You will gradually change friends and change attitudes and change the kinds of places you hang out in. The Lord will begin to talk to you day by day. He'll begin to work out the old and bring in the new and pretty soon you'll be consumed with the light, that glorious light. It starts with a decision. You may not feel a thing, but I guarantee that if you grab it by faith, something internal will begin to happen and begin to function in your life.

Chapter Three

Feeding the Hunger

When you are physically hungry, your insides start screaming and rattling, saying, "I want something to eat—now!"

When there is a spiritual hunger, there is a desire way down deep inside that you can't explain. When you realize you've already eaten everything in the house and you still have a void, your mind turns towards God's Word. When there's a spiritual hunger on the inside, it is the makings of one miserable being on the outside. I believe there are a lot of spiritually hungry people. Can I say this to you in all honesty? I would rather have twenty-five or thirty spiritually hungry folks come into our church than to have four or five hundred who don't give a hoot about the things of God. If there is a void in your life, through the Word, God can minister to you.

Could we be honest with each other? I'm finding out for myself that this thing called *Christianity* is more than just saying, "I prayed a prayer once upon a time; now I'm saved." No, you're really not saved until something different—something drastically different—happens on the inside. It is an internal matter. It is not about what we look like on the outside. I can put on a suit and have my big fat smile on when I get to church, but you will know by the time I walk out that door if that smile is for real. You'll know what's on the inside. We can all put on a front, but God wants us to be real and honest. He wants to hear us say, "I'm hungry and I need to know more about you, God. What I thought was the Christian life, I'm finding out is much different. I'm finding that at different places of my Christian walk it is much more difficult than I ever thought it would be."

To be a true Christian, we need God to come in and change our lives. We need Him to change our minds. We need God to show us something no man has ever seen. It's not a man thing; it's a God thing. We have been fooled into believing that praying the sinner's prayer is all there is to it. We have believed that for so long, but we haven't felt that anything happened on the inside. Now we find ourselves somewhere in this thing called "the Christian Walk," and we're confused about God. We were told that God is right there in our midst, but I'll tell you, I can't see God for the life of me.

Have you ever reached out to try to see God or feel God? You hear preachers say "Just reach out and touch him," and you're steadily trying to touch Him, but you don't feel a thing. That is because we put so much on the natural level. God is not a natural God. John 4:24 tells us God is a spirit, and they that worship Him must worship Him in spirit and in truth. That tells me something on the inside has to happen before I'm going to start feeling Him on the inside. I know He's working on the outside when I can walk up and shake your hand, hug your neck, share a word with you, and know that God has touched you through my life. Have you ever tried to witness, only to go home discouraged and confused and frustrated because once upon a time a preacher told you, "You prayed that prayer and now you can just go out and be a witness"? You better have something to be a witness about.

God-based Living

I have lived a large part of my life based on what other men said. I thought my good friend was teaching me about marriage, only to find out he would tear my home apart quicker than the devil himself. I've lived too long listening to the money man teach me how to make a dollar, only to find that he was a fraud. I know that Christ resides in my life, but I've lived too long based on what somebody else told me about Christ. Now, I've got to know for myself. I have to know what the Word is saying when it says, "If any man be in Christ."

I'm finding that I've just been holding on to Christ for thirty-five years. Some of us, I believe, are finding we've just been holding on. How can you know if you are one of those who have been holding on? If you're holding on to the word *Christian*—to the covering of that prayer—that's a pretty good indication that you're holding on to Christ. "If any man be in Christ, he is a new creature." He said "Behold, all things are become new." That means I don't think the way I used to think. I don't hide behind the spiritual curtain like I used to. I tell you, I can raise my hand and preach and teach with the best of them. I can pick up trash, mow the lawn, and clean the carpet with the best of them. I can dress with the best and drive with the best. I can go out and eat with the best. But that means about what it did when a little boy saw the preacher take his watch off and lay it on the podium. The boy asked, "Pastor, what does it mean when you lay your watch up on the podium?" He said "Son, it doesn't mean a thing." Because if any man has truly found Christ, he won't rationalize, "I'm going to spend my money on the church, and then, hopefully, God will be there for me when I need Him."

Every one of you who desires to be a true believer is going to have to let the old things go away. I don't care if you have been in this thing called "the Christian Walk" for ninety-nine years; there are some things we need to let go of.

The person who has truly repented and changed his ways is simply a person who has seen Christ. I'm not talking about seeing Christ in the natural. Look at 1 John 2:15. (Whenever you read a scripture passage, be it two or three or a dozen verses, always read what is said before and what is said after so that you can get the full picture. Don't just pick out one verse.) It says, "Love not the world, neither the things that are in the world. If any man love the world, the love of the father is not in him."

I had someone not long ago say, "Pastor, I smoke and I have a drink occasionally, and I don't feel any guilt over it. I actually enjoy it. But I'm a Christian, and I thank God for what He's done in my life." How can you enjoy the love of the world, and enjoy the love of Christ at the same time? Revelation 3:15 says, "I wish you were either hot or cold." We send mixed signals when we claim to be one thing but live another. Verses 16 and 17 of 1 John 2 are very specific. "For all that is in the world, the lust of the flesh, and the lust of the eyes, and the pride of life, is not of the father, but is of the world. And the world passeth away, and the lust thereof, but he that doeth the will of God abideth forever." You cannot be live-in partners and say you have a godly nature. There comes a time when there has to be a separation.

Growth Takes Time

God will help you pick out things in your life that are wrong and then, because of His grace and mercy, He will give you an opportunity to change those things. As much as God is a "right now" God and He wants to see righteousness right now, God understands that it took some of us many years to get in the condition we're in. But through day-by-day sanctification, we can begin to change our attitudes. Aren't you glad God doesn't expect us to be like a genie and *Boing*, we're changed?

People ask, "How is it that I can be prayed for and feel an immediate difference?" Because you've made a decision to follow Christ. You made a decision not to be the person you were yesterday. But too often we've hidden behind the cross by saying, "I've prayed the prayer, so I know I'm a Christian, but I still do what I've always done." That is not a true Christian. That is not what the Word teaches us. You don't give an offering just because the plates are passing by. You give with a passion and with a reason, not because the preacher is watching. You give because you feel something in your heart, and you know God has blessed you with what you have. Because of that, you want to share with God. I want to give what I've got because Acts 20:35 tells me it's more blessed to give. It seems the more I give, the more I get. But if you're giving to get, then stop giving. It's the wrong reason.

I read a tee shirt recently that said, "The world thinks Christians should be committed" (meaning "put away"), then the bottom line said "and so does God." God thinks we should be committed, not in the jail or the loony bin, but we should be committed to our faith. We can't be committed to faith just by saying we prayed a prayer. The world says if any man pray a prayer, he's a free man. That is not what my Bible told me. My Bible says if any man be in Christ, he's a new creature. How can I get *in* to someone I know nothing about?

Do you know why many marriages don't last? Because we get into lust. "Wow, that looks nice. Wow, I'm in love overnight." No, you're not; you're in lust. Our marriages would last if we would get together out of love. Our church families would be so much stronger if we would get together in love. This whole thing is a walk of faith. Ministry is faith. By faith it's going to grow and people are going to come in. By faith you receive the Word. By faith, when you pray the prayer of repentance, you're going to receive Christ in a way and a manner that you've never received Him. You will go out and encourage others.

When you come to God with an attitude that says, "I'm going to get what I can and to heck with all the rest," you'll never receive a thing. All some people want is to receive the Holy Ghost. You need to receive Jesus before you worry about the Holy Ghost.

There are all kinds of sin out there. There are all kinds of junk we have allowed to attach to our lives, and now we find ourselves in bondage. We find out we've just been holding on to Christ. We can't love the things of the world. We can't just go with a passion. When we truly get in Christ, we will recognize the devil when he walks through the doors. You've seen that pretty thing up there on the billboard, sitting on a horse and smoking a cigarette. That's a pretty devil. When we get in Christ, we are able to discern what comes through the door. Too often we allow ourselves to live in the flesh.

How do we know when we're not in Christ? Because we have the nature and the mind of the world. Do, do, do. Go, go, go. Get, get, get. Take, take, take. James 1:19 says we should be slow to speak and very quick to listen. If you are in Christ, there is never a day that God won't talk to you and deal with you about the kind of person you are. Does it mean you're a bad person if God is always having to straighten you out? No, you're a bad person if you won't let Him straighten you out. You're a hypocrite if you come in and out of church, week in and week out, and a year later you're still doing the things you were a year ago.

The Bible says that if I have faults, I should go to my brothers and say, "I have a fault." We need that kind of peace in the house of God. We need a real freedom to come and say, "Would you pray with me?" That's where brotherly love comes together. If any man be in Christ, he has a brother and a sister in the Lord. If any man be in Christ, he has received God; he has gained God as father.

At one time all of us have prayed, "Hey stranger, hey God, are you really out there?" But when something happens inside my heart, I know that even in the midst of turmoil, God is here. That's where my smile comes from. That's where my joy comes from. Oh, on the outside I may be hurting. On the outside I may have a lot of fear. On the outside I may be bound. I may not have the money for the doctor. I may not know how I'm going to make it through next week, next month. I don't know how I'm going to send my kids to school. I don't know how my husband or my wife is going to stay with me for another six months. I don't know how I'm going to make it. I may be in shambles on the outside, but I can guarantee you if any man be in Christ, we'll take Him at His Word. We'll believe that God said He would not allow more to come on us than we are able to bear (1 Cor. 10:13). If we're going to call ourselves *believers*, there comes a time when we must take God at His Word.

Our Position in Christ

Some of us are going to have to take the cross and get it out of the way—because we've been hiding behind it. We're going to have to face the cross. In a general sense, we are the offspring of God the Creator. Acts 17:28–29 says:

> For in him we live, and move, and have our being; as certain of your own poets have said, for we are also his offspring. Forasmuch then as we are the offspring of God, we ought not to think that the Godhead is like unto gold, or silver, or stone, graven by art and man's device.

Can I say it this way? If we are His offspring and if in Him we live and move and have our being, then we're not going to look at God as a source for gold or for silver. If you are not in Christ, you may stand up and say, "God helped me get financing and I got a new vehicle," and then when the first payment is due you may stand up and say, "God cursed me." He either blessed you or He cursed you, but He's not going to do both. He's not an Indian giver. He's not going to give so He can take. It is man's nature to be an Indian giver.

I have a chandelier sitting in the storage trailer out back that someone bought—supposedly paid hundreds of dollars for—and donated to a church he attended once upon a time. When he got mad and left that church, he took his doggoned chandelier down and said, "It's mine, and I'm taking it with me." Then he came to our church and said, "I want you to hang it." What, so you can come and rip it out of this ceiling, too?

I've had folks say recently, "I've donated money for a particular cause, and now that my calling is not upon this ministry any longer, I want it back. And if you don't give it back, you're going to have to deal with God." Either we're in Christ or we're not. Either I love my wife with a passion or I don't. Either I am in love with the one who created me or I am just a stinking coward.

America has become a "try it out" society. Try marriage. If it doesn't work, try someone else. I heard of somebody who had been married fifteen times. I thought, *Dear mercy*. I remember the first ten years of our marriage. We stayed in one place for four years, but we moved twenty times. During the first twelve years we were married, I traded vehicles twenty-eight times. If any man be in Christ, stability begins to happen. My mind begins to change. I get to where what people say about me doesn't affect me the way it used to.

Sometimes people come and say, "God didn't really heal you of leukemia. That was luck." I tell you, there was no luck charm, piece of gold or silver or graven calf that walked into my hospital room and healed me. It took an internal happening. It took a spirit. And since the enemy hates my guts, he's not going to heal me. God came in His spirit and love and entered into this being. He took out the dead blood cells, and replaced them with new, fresh, living blood cells.

I love it when doctors say they want to check my blood. "Sure," I say, "Peck away and check all you want. Take a gallon; I don't care."

They say, "That's some of the prettiest blood we've ever seen."

"That's God's blood. Do you want some?"

If any man be in Christ, he's a new creature.

Give Yourself a Check-up

Why do you go to church? Because it is Sunday? After you walk through the doors, does your reason change for being there? Have you called yourself a believer for three, four, five, thirty, forty, fifty, sixty years? Are there areas of your life where you've just been holding on, but now it's time to know more about this Jesus?

When I see the battles and trials my wife walks through on my behalf, it makes a tear want to well up because I know that she's in me and I'm in her. I see her tears, the stability, and the boldness that comes on that woman when the devil starts coming against her. She can just twitch, and I know what she's about to say. You haven't enjoyed a Christlike life until you can hear Christ Himself get ready to speak to you. "Son, I want you to go and bless my brother." He speaks to you on such a still, small level.

But God is not a confusing God. You don't have to go to church and then go home wondering, "Am I saved?" You can go home knowing that if He comes back before you get home, you are going with Him. You can know that it doesn't matter how much money you do or don't have. It doesn't matter what you drove to church or how you're going to get to work tomorrow. What matters is that God knows something has come alive on the inside. You don't want to miss what God is saying. God is beginning to light your fire because He loves you.

If any man be in Christ, his attitude changes. When you get in the right frame of mind, you begin to walk the path that Christ walked when they cursed Him, stomped Him, persecuted Him, pierced His side, and beat Him like a dog. One of the times that cat-o'-nine-tails came down across His back, it had my name on it. The Father knew I was going to be eaten up with leukemia. And the Savior, the great physician, took the pain and the suffering and wore my stripes that I would someday find healing. He wore my name. Today He wears my name, and whatever ailment comes my way—difficulties in my marriage, finances, or children—doesn't matter because He wore the stripes. He loves you. He gave His life that you might live. In Him I live and move and have my being. In

Him, I'm a new creature. The outward may be perishing, but the inward is being renewed day by day.

If you feel the Lord tugging at your heart, tell Him what you're feeling. If you have a physical, mental, financial, marital, or any other condition that only God Himself can work on your behalf, talk to Him about it. He'll show you what it is to be in Christ—regardless of your circumstances. The Lord is so loving and so caring. He has your best interests in mind.

Chapter Four

It All Starts with Birth

When God healed me of leukemia, He gave me a new bloodline. A new bloodline means you live and don't have to die. I'm talking in the natural and the spiritual. God can take your condition and build you up. He can recreate you and make you what He designed you for. I thank God for showing me the difference between being of God and in God. Don't come to me with a frown on your face saying you've been changed. I won't believe you. When you're changed and are truly in Christ, you are a new creature.

It's like when you buy a new automobile. You don't have to tell someone you're driving something different. They notice. You don't have to tell someone you have a new suit of clothes. They recognize they've never seen that before. Neither do you have to tell anyone you've found Christ in a brand new way; it is evident.

It's apparent by the way you live and the conversation you keep. How many of you have some stuff you would like God to take? I'm not talking in the natural. If you look in my garage, my wife will tell you there's some stuff that needs to go. We all have stuff, but I'm talking spiritually. There's stuff—old things, old ways of thinking, junk—that has to go.

Do you ever get tired of being "the same old person"? Do you ever get tired of grumbling about the same old thing? I do. I say, "Lord, change that about me." But sometimes, I say, "Lord, why does it matter if the grass in the yard is a foot deep? I'm still going to heaven." When it rains a lot, I'm going to have to cut the grass. That's just the way it is. But why should I gripe about it? Where's my peace; where's my joy? Who is my life in? Is my life so shallow that because the lawn is deep, I lose my joy and peace?

People come to church happy because the news is great, it is nice and cool inside, and it's a wonderful day. But as soon as they walk out the door, they lose their joy because it's too hot. At certain times of the year, the Lord lets us get chilly, and then we gripe because it's too cold. We need to get in Christ. I don't care how hot or how cold it is.

I found my Savior. I have located someone who has made himself a part of my internal life, and now I don't worry about what tomorrow holds. I could care less if tomorrow even gets here. It's not going to change my faith. It doesn't really matter if yesterday wants to haunt me. It's not going to change my future. We can't change yesterday, but we can sure change tomorrow.

Out with the Old

If any man be in Christ, he's a brand new creature. Maybe you should speak those words aloud, so your heart will take notice. Sometimes you need to talk to yourself. Sometimes you need to get a song in your heart and say "Lord, let your spirit rise up within me." Other times, you need to say, "Lord, I'm confused and baffled today. I don't know what decisions to make or where I should go. But God, let something spring up that's been deposited down in my spirit so my mind will be straightened out." We talk to ourselves about all the bad things that happen. We need to start telling ourselves about all the good. I can tell you plenty of bad news, but I'm not going to concentrate my time on what's bad. Because after I've concentrated on it, guess what? It's still going to be bad. But when I find Jesus and I find myself in Him and He finds Himself in me, I'm a brand new creature.

It doesn't matter what the world, the neighbor, or the dog thinks. I've found something and I'm different. And guess what? He'll make you a new creature every day. I can pray and repent every day. Every day I can find a brand new revelation that will make me fresh all over. It makes the devil sick when you get in the Book and start finding things out for yourself. I can be out in the middle of the desert, where there is not a soul to be found, but I've still got victory. I have joy springing up from deep within, and I have something to sing about. That is the difference between having something in your head and having something in your heart.

I have to be honest with you about my marriage. When we were first married, I said I loved my wife because all I knew about love was enough to say I loved her. But I've found, seventeen years later, that love is a bit different than I thought it was. I say I love my children, but wait until they wake me up at one o'clock in the morning and something is wrong. I say I love God but what about when He wakes me out of a dead sleep? Somebody called me bright and early one Monday morning. I was tired. At ten minutes to seven the phone rang and someone said, "Preacher, would you pray for me?" My natural man wanted to say, "Pray for yourself." But something inside me said, *Mind, shut up. Get out of bed, go to the other room, and pray.*

True Christians are Givers

If any man be in Christ, he's a giver, not a taker. We know we are the offspring of God because Ephesians 2:10 says we are His workmanship. Just because we are His workmanship does not cover up the fact that we need an intimate relationship with Christ. We can't just say, "He made me; He's my creator, so that's all I need." It's more than praying a prayer. It's digging into the Word and saying, "Lord, exactly what are you saying to me?" Something miraculous has to happen. A transformation has to take place. If you've never had life-shaking, earth-shattering transformation, then I suggest you go back to the drawing board and say, "Father, I want to feel what I'm believing. I'm tired of claiming I'm a Christian because somebody told me I was. I'm tired of not feeling anything when everyone else is weeping before you."

There is a difference between being in Christ and being of Christ. My children hold on to me because I supply their needs. But when they come in with no motive other than to snuggle with me on the couch and say, "I love you," that is something entirely different. They love me because of who I am and not because of what I can give them. Until we become believers who love others for who they are and not for what they can give us, then we'll never be the people of God we need to be. It is a disgrace when we see people only in terms of what they can do for us. We could think things like, *Oh, he's a tree cutter. If I buy him lunch, maybe he'll cut a tree for nothing.* Or we could say things like, "I'm so grateful that you came by today. If you never come back again, it meant something to me that you did come," and really mean it.

Starting Over

Have you ever wished you could be born again? That you could do some parts of your life over? I'll be honest. There are times I look back and think, *Boy, did I mess up.* I didn't have to go bankrupt to find that God was God. He could have kept me out of bankruptcy, but I wouldn't listen. I didn't have to have all those unnecessary fights with my family. You know what happens after a big fight? You find out that you're the one who needs to change.

Sometimes I tell my wife "the way it is." Two days later, I'm out there changing, but I'm not going to say I was wrong. Makes me sick. Finally, I have to say, "I am so sorry. I did not mean to say what I did."

She'll say, "I guess I didn't mean those things either." Then we can go on from there together.

John 3:3 says, "Jesus answered and said unto him, 'Verily, verily I say unto thee, Except a man be born again, he cannot see the kingdom of God.'" When one receives Christ as Savior, he is born into a new spiritual family. That's why we should not forsake the gathering and assembling together of believers. We have a new family. I have a new father, God the Father. But not only is God my Father but also He is my Daddy. I can say, "Daddy, I need you," just like I can go to my earthly father and say the same. He's the one I can commune with, and the one who talks to me.

When this new birth is genuine, I also gain brothers and sisters in the Lord. A few weeks ago a friend called me and said, "What's going on?"

I said, "What do you mean, what's going on?"

"I just thought you might need a friend," he said.

Thank God for friends like that. It's one thing for a friend to see what they can get from you. It's another thing for a friend to say, "I just wanted to visit with you."

When you are in Christ, you gain. You gain friends in the Lord and Christ as Father. You can drive down the road and say, "Father, please intervene. I need you." You can call a friend in the Lord and say, "I need to talk to you." You can walk through the grocery store and see another believer and know they believe as you do.

A good friend stopped by one day, and I shared with him what I've been learning about the characteristics of true Christianity. He told me his father had been a preacher his whole life and that now his father was old, miserable, and in pain. He can't wait to get off the face of this earth. My friend said, "As much as I love my Daddy, and as much as I love the way my Daddy believed, he missed some things." What he was saying is that his Dad doesn't have to be miserable and wretched. He can be happy and joyful in spite of the circumstances.

If we're not careful, we can miss that Christians can come together on a Friday night and have ice cream and there isn't any sin in it. My friend said, "I have a hard time being part of a church because I get tired of people trying to tell me how to live. Why can't they just tell me how to be in Christ and let me choose for myself who I am going to serve?"

I decided some time ago that I will no longer tell my congregation, "I am going to change you." Instead, I am going to love them and share my heart with them. If they receive it, I'm going to love them. If they reject it, I'm still going to love them. My job is to teach; change is God's job. If any man be in Christ, he's a new creature.

The New Birth

The natural birth is an initiation to a new experience of life for the parents. From the moment a woman finds out she's going to become a mother, everything changes about the way she thinks and lives. Suddenly she becomes a giver and not a taker. A new process has begun. Eighteen days after the seed is conceived, the baby's heart begins to beat. By twenty-one days, it's pumping through a closed circulatory system, meaning the baby has a blood whose type is different from that of the mother. At forty days, brain waves have been recorded. At six and a half weeks, all twenty milk teeth buds are present. At six to seven weeks, the baby can move. By eight weeks all body systems are present, and by eleven weeks, all are working. At eleven to twelve weeks, the baby is breathing fluids steadily and continues to until birth. Fingernails are present at eleven to twelve weeks. Eyelashes are present by sixteen weeks. And as you know, by around nine months, there's a brand new child, a brand new creation, something that everybody is just thrilled about.

People say they long for the Church of old, but the Church of old was a giving church. I remember the weekend of a church dedication in Ocala, Florida. My dad and one or two other men took a pickup truck and shovels and went out to the cow pasture to dig up sod so there would be grass in front of the new church building on dedication day. You ask someone today to come out and pull a weed out of the flowerbed, and they'll tell you what they think of you.

When we're *of* Christ rather than *in* Christ, we accept and take for granted all the benefits of Christ. We wear our Christian shirts and show up on Sunday and give our offerings. We have the appearance of Christ, but the truth comes out when someone asks, "Could you give me an hour of your time?"

"You know I'd love to," we say. "It's in my heart, but I have to go fishing."

There are some principles of the Church of old that we've left. We are going to have to go back and pick them up if we are going to teach this generation how to be people that are in Christ, not merely of Christ.

I find it quite interesting that a spiritual birth comes after one has heard and received the Word of God. You can't experience new birth until you have been taught. You have to learn the Word. You have to know what "For all have sinned and come short of the glory of God" means (Rom. 3:23). We get saved through the

Word. We grow through the Word. The Word shows us how to fight off the enemy. Ephesians 6:13 tells us we need the sword of the spirit. Ephesians 5:18 tells us to sing spiritual songs. But I didn't know about that weapon until I got into the Word. If you're feeling lonely, sing "What a Friend We Have in Jesus." God doesn't care if you can't carry a tune in a bucket. If you're in need, tell the Lord. I didn't know about salvation until I got into the Word. Neither did I know about the weapons for fighting the enemy until I got into the Word. In here are hidden truths. Seek out the Word; seek and find.

How do you know if you have genuinely been saved? The tune in your heart will change before you get to the door. Suddenly, movies that were OK before now make you uncomfortable. You feel bad about saying certain things and about having certain friends. It's called *conviction*. You can't learn how to serve Christ unless you get in the Word.

James 1:21 says, "Wherefore lay apart all filthiness and superfluity and naughtiness and receive with meekness the engrafted Word, which is able to save your souls." First Peter 1:23 tells us, "Being born again, not of corruptible seed, but of incorruptible, by the Word of God, which liveth and abideth forever." We must learn to listen and to be slow to speak. Someone said it is better to be thought a fool than to speak and remove all doubt. So many times in my life I wish I had just left it alone. By the words I spoke, they knew I was a fool. When Christ is beginning to get in us and we're getting in Christ, we need to sit patiently, quietly, and listen with our spirits. I hate it when people ask me, "Are you a Christian?" I want them to come up and say, "I know you're a child of God" because they see something different in me.

Salvation and growth are not human accomplishments but acts of God. Quit trying to be saved. Quit trying to change your life.

I spoke to a gentleman who said he had two or three hundred thousand dollars in the bank, and he had lost thirty thousand dollars gambling with it. I asked him, "Why don't you throw your money away to the Church if you are going to throw it away?"

He said, "I might come back and talk to you, but I want you to understand something. I know I can't give my way into somewhere special. There is a God and it's between me and Him."

You can't buy God's love; He gives it freely. John 1:13 says, "Which were born, not of blood, or the will of the flesh, nor of the will of man, but of God." Ephesians 2:8 says, "For by grace are ye saved through faith; and that not of yourselves: it is the gift of God." James 1:18 tells us, "Of his own will begat he us with the Word of truth, that we should be a kind of first fruits of his creatures." New birth cannot happen alone. You don't do it by yourself. God needs you as much as you need Him for new birth to happen.

New birth comes through repentance and obedience to the Word you have received. Everything that happens through Christ happens through our obedience. He can share His love and give His life on the cross, but if I don't receive it and if I'm not obedient to His Word, it means nothing. I can put a down payment on a car, but if I don't go back to pick it up, it means nothing. I'm still going to walk.

Romans 2:11 tells us that God is no respecter of persons. If He saved me, He will save you. If He healed me, He will heal you. If He blessed me, He will bless you. We must quit looking at ourselves as something other than what we are. God loves us, and He sent His Son to die for us.

Before you go to bed tonight, ask the Lord to forgive you for whatever wrong was in your life today. It's nothing new to God. If you really want to be in Christ, ask Him to straighten out the areas of your life you can't straighten out on your own. There comes a time when you have to do something about what the Lord has said to us. You have to get yourself to the place of obedience. If He has been tugging at your heart, listen to what He is saying. If you let Him, He will come in and make you what He wants you to be—not what you think you should be.

Chapter Five

Intimate Change

This is just a moment, a piece of dust taking up space. My hope is not in being here tomorrow. My security, my dream, and my vision are in knowing I have received Jesus Christ as Lord and Savior. Before He died on the cross, the Romans cursed Him, bruised Him, stomped on Him, and beat Him to a pulp. At any moment, Jesus could have said, "No more for me." Thank God He didn't back off. He didn't change His mind. We don't serve a coward. Our God is a giver. Too many believers, though, say, "That's enough. No more for me. Lord, you brought me this far, but I'm not going any further." What a tragedy. They nailed Christ to the cross so you and I could admit there is sin in our lives and ask for forgiveness. We may have different sins, but sin is sin and wrong is wrong. But, thank God, redemption is redemption, and the blood is the blood.

First Corinthians 15:52 reminds us that someday there is going to be a trumpet sound. Even though the world says we should be depressed and totally out of our minds because of the pressures of life, God says, "*Hold on to me and see what I'll do for you. You're here for only a moment.*"

I hear a lot of different sounds, but there is one in particular I'm tuned into and waiting to hear. Old Gabriel is going to blow that trumpet, and when he does, we are going to meet Christ. What a day, what a day it's going to be. No more sin, no more pain, no more heartache, no more frustration.

How can you be assured of that day? Give your heart to Jesus. Give up your will to Him and get in Him and let Him get in you.

But, at the same time, make the most of the time we have here. The world needs young men and ladies who will stay pure. The world needs children, teenagers, and adults who will love the Lord with their whole hearts. Every person has a talent and a gift. We can choose to let that gift be used or we can wait until we are thirty, fifty, or eighty and then look back and regret the wasted time.

Keep your trust in God, not in people. Friends, even family sometimes, will turn their backs on you. But no matter who lets you down, Jesus is still going to be there every step of the way. He says in His Word, "I'll never leave you, or forsake you, and I'll stick closer than a brother" (Heb. 13:5 paraphrased). I put my faith and my hope in that. No matter how many times I fail, He's going to be there. Jesus will always, always, always, always be there.

Know the Word

Too many believers yell, scream, whoop, and holler only to come back to earth and find themselves unable to stand because they do not have knowledge of the Word. The Bible tells us to be strong in the Word so we can withstand in the evil day. We are living in the evil day, and we have an enemy. First Peter 5:8 tells us that everyone who accepts Christ has an adversary.

The enemy hates you so much he will do everything he can to deceive you and take away the word that has been given. The Bible says the enemy comes immediately; he doesn't wait a week or two. You might think, *God blessed me and I'll be ready to face the enemy six weeks from now.* No, you better be ready right now because he hates you right now. If the enemy can't pull you back, he will try to push you overboard. Some folks think, *I'm so spiritual, I only need God once every two months or so.* Wrong.

In 2 Corinthians 5:17, the Word tells us to be in Christ, not of Christ. It will never be enough to say, "I experienced Him once upon a time. I know that Christ is the one who came and healed my land." This Scripture does not say, "If any man be in Christ, he's an old creature." The Word says, "If any man be in Christ, he's a brand new creature." There is something different. It should be so apparent that total strangers will walk up to us and say, "There is something different about you."

Often we don't understand that God uses our individual lives to reach other individuals. During the years I have been privileged to lead folks in the Lord, I've been guilty of leading on the surface. When you begin to search your life, you realize it's not about what you know. It's about whether or not you know Christ and how well you know Him. It doesn't matter where you come from, what your training is, or who your mama or daddy is. Someday you must ask yourself, "Is my view of Christ based on what the preacher told me about Christ, or is my view of Christ something I've experienced? Do I have a relationship with Christ that the preacher can't take away from me?"

When something intimate has happened, nobody can take that from you. God healed me of leukemia. I don't care if you like it or if you even believe it. I'm not here to debate what has God has done for me.

There comes a time when we have to get in Christ, become that new creature, and know where we stand and whom we trust. Many of us have called ourselves believers based on what someone in the pulpit told us about whom we believe in. It is time to get in the Word and know for ourselves what we believe and whom we believe in. Someone who bases his or her faith in a preacher is going to have real problems if that preacher leaves the church. Your faith must be between you and God.

In order to be in Christ, a birth has to take place. In John 3 we read that Nicodemus came to Jesus after the sun went down. Could it have been because he didn't want anyone to see him? Possibly, but the point is that he came. It doesn't matter when or where you come to Jesus. It could be at night, by day, in winter, in summer, at the mall, in the field, in your automobile, or at church. It simply doesn't matter where or when. What matters is that you come to Him with a heart of repentance. Jesus said, "Verily, verily, I say unto thee, except a man be born again, he cannot see the kingdom of God." When Nicodemus asked how a man could enter into his mother's womb when he is old and be born again, the Lord said, "That which is born of spirit is spirit, and that which is born of flesh is flesh." The new birth is a spiritual thing. Come to Christ, no matter where you are. Just come. He is waiting to hear from you.

No Band-Aids

Every person must get beyond what he knows of Christ and begin to live for Him by what he receives—by that touch on the inner man. I know when the inner man has been touched because I feel the spirit. There are tears that come from the head and then there are the tears that come from a broken heart. When there is trouble at home between husband and wife or parents and children, the tears come from way down in the heart.

Every person has some area down deep that hurts. But for that kind of hurt, you can't go into the house of God, gain a little knowledge of Christ and His Word, and then put a Band-Aid on your head and say, "OK, my hurt is healed." The Band-Aid may make you feel better for a day or two, but after that, it gets full of germs and you have to change it. A Band-Aid of knowledge won't change your heart. You can't live by what you know in your head; you're going to have to get that knowledge down into your heart. You're going to have to allow something intimate to happen between you and Christ.

You know you've been saved because something's happened on the inside, and you begin to think and to see things differently. You realize that people aren't your enemies. The Bible didn't say that your congregation, your husband, or your wife is going to come against you. The Word says, "Your adversary, the devil. The evil one." He's coming.

When I allow myself to begin to get in Christ, I feel that new creature beginning to rise up because now I don't see God's people as the enemy. I see people whom God loves, who are in the same boat I'm in. We're all striving for the same trumpet sound. Some of us sit like the great saints of God, but we really don't see anything.

When you come to Christ in faith, He comes in power. When you have faith and power mixed all together, you've got something worth holding on to.

What Are You Doing?

When repentance comes, this thing the Word calls *new birth* happens. Years ago, people got all excited when a new baby was born. These days, we say, "Who cares?" We've gotten so wrapped up in life and become so religious that we have forgotten how to be intimate with people. We have forgotten that if any man be in Christ, he acts differently, responds differently, and receives others differently. On the road to Damascus, the Lord said to Paul, "Why do you persecute me?"

If the Lord hasn't approached you yet, hold on because He's about to. And when He does, He's going to call you by name and ask, "Why do you do the things you do?" You will have to do more than say, "I don't know." The Lord will begin saying, "This, this, and this is wrong in your life, but let me help you. I will show you how I can be in you and you can be in me." When He showed Paul those things, Paul disappeared for several years. When he came back, the religious leaders wanted to murder him because he had a powerful word.

When you become a new creature—somebody different—the world is not going to understand. They won't understand why you are joyful while they are frowning, upset, and brokenhearted.

You may read this and think, *I've served God for fifteen years, but I don't understand what you're talking about.* That is my point, exactly. We've gone from the decision, "OK, Lord, I repent," all the way to the shout. There are lots of us shouting, but we don't know what we're shouting about. We're shouting because sister Suzy's shouting. Where does real, true repentance begin? We can't change the world until we change ourselves. I can't come and minister to you until something happens at home. And I can't even change my home until something happens in me. Too often we don't teach that. We just say, "Come pray. Show up every now and then and pay your tithe and praise God. You'll be just fine."

You better wake up, Christian. You better get in the Word and see that the Word says, "If any man be in Christ, he's a new creature." He doesn't act the way that he used to act. His old principles, his old habits, his old ways are totally different.

We have been told that if you smoke, drink, or cuss, you're going to hell and that if you receive Christ, everything is happy, life is wonderful, and you are joyful ever after. So we say, "I won't smoke, drink, or cuss because I don't want to go to hell." The problem is the other ninety-nine billion sins.

I just knew that if I didn't smoke, drink, or cuss, I was going to heaven and that if I accepted Christ, everything would be joyful, happy, and precious. Nobody ever told me I needed God's Word because the moment I accepted Christ and made a decision to serve Him, the enemy would come to mess with my head. He meets you at the church door and says, "You didn't really get saved. Don't be stupid. Don't go out there and tell anybody you met a Christ you can't even see."

Well, what do you do with your life at that moment? You need to get in the Word so you'll know what to hang on to and what to let go of. According to 1 John 2:27, when the Holy Spirit comes, you don't need any man to teach you. You just need the Father. It is time to quit believing every little thing that comes your way. You are going to have to go to the Word and research some of the things you've been taught all these years.

Someone came to me the other day and said, "I've served God for forty-five years, but I found there are areas where I am definitely not in Christ, and I always thought I was." If any man be in Christ, he may look the same on the outside, but something is being renewed on the inside.

When the people of Israel were about to choose a king, God said to Samuel in essence, "You're considering a man who looks mighty fine with his nice hair and muscular build, but I want you to know that I look at men differently. I look at what's on the inside" (see 1 Sam. 15:7). It is not what's on the outside that counts.

When a person has been spiritually awakened, you can't put them to sleep. You can't shut them up either. I heard of a preacher who got in the Word and got to preaching it, and suddenly, every time he turned around, some of the saints were up in the trees and out on a limb about to go crazy in order to do something for Christ. He said the people showed up one night with blocks of two-by-fours to play as instruments before the Lord. I would like to get some of our people up the tree!

When something begins to happen in your heart, you may find that divorce is not what you need. You will begin to look at the good inside the person you are with. A new job may not be what you need. A new church may not be what you need. A new God may not be what you need. God's concern is not how well we look on the outside. His concern is what is going on inside. Let God kill out the old. Let Him kill out the poison and change your attitude.

One gentleman said, "Just as soon as I clean up my life, I'm going to come to Christ."

I said, "Do you clean up before you take a bath? Of course not. You just get in the way you are. We come to Christ the same way."

Pick out some areas in your life that the Lord needs to change. Maybe you have relied on what the preacher says about faith for too long. It is time to find out about this thing called Christianity on your own. Preachers come and go. Churches come and go. Doctors come and go. We need something to stand by. We need something to base our lives on. The characteristics of true Christianity are so different from what I perceived them to be. We need to get into the Word and find out what He is saying to us.

Recently, a member of our congregation lost his battle with cancer and went to be with the Lord. The doctors had given him every kind of medication and had done everything they knew to do. He had been in five different hospitals in two months. But every place he went and every chance he got, he shared Jesus. I prayed with him and then said, "Brother George, now I want you to pray for me." I could not clearly understand his words, but the man took his time even though he only had a few more hours to live. Brother George was a new creature. He knew God and he made no bones about it. I watched him minister to nurse after nurse, doctor after doctor, planting seeds. Here was a man who was dying, leaving this world praying. Afterwards, I thought, *God, let me see what Brother George sees.*

You are going to have to get on the inside of Christ. You're going to have to quit relying on what you know. All the education in the world can't take you to glory. They say many people will miss heaven by eighteen inches—the distance between their heads and their hearts. Ask God to get inside you and begin to change you from the inside out. Get in the Word every day, and ask Him to show you how to go from being of Christ to living each day in Christ.

Chapter Six

Growing in Grace

It takes obedience for a person to get out of self and into Christ. It's by obedience that Christ changed my life. Not only did I have to hear the Word but also I had to respond to the Word. I responded out of obedience as a child to my father's command.

Obedience to Christ brings great results. It seems that if I take a step, Christ will take two steps. Have you ever noticed that when you take a step to be obedient to Christ financially, it seems He will walk a mile? When you say, "I'm just going to worship Him," something happens inside?

If you are the same person you have always been, you are not the kind of Christian I'm talking about. You are not the person I'm looking for. The Word says in Luke that He gave me power to believe. He gave me power to receive. He gave me power to respond to His command and call. He gave me that power so I could be obedient to His Word. When I was obedient, I gave my life to Christ, and the new birth happened. Something new, something different, something great. Thank God, I'm a new creature in Christ.

Paul said, "I would not have you ignorant concerning the things of God" (1 Cor. 12:1, paraphrased). We're going to have to get in Christ for ourselves. We are going to have to allow the new birth to take place.

Growth Takes Time

In my opinion, here's what is wrong with the Church today: there are too many folks who have gone from 0 to 140 overnight. Let me put it this way: we know a gentleman who loves racing. When he decided to get involved himself, instead of starting off with the "little boys," he jumped right in there with the "big boys." The first time we saw him race, he tore the wall all to pieces. Why? Because he was in an arena that he shouldn't have been in yet. Why is it that Christians rise up and then fall? Because they're born again, genuinely born again, but then they never take time to be fed by milk and then by bread.

I remember leaving our child one day with a babysitter. Our child was still too young for table food, but when we came home, we found her with a chicken bone in her mouth. I yelled, "Dear God, you're choking my child! I thought you were my friend."

The babysitter said, "I'm just trying to get her used to table food."

That is what often happens in the Church. People get saved and then we stick a bone in their mouths too soon and they choke. And when they choke, they end up hurt and offended. Proverbs 18:19 says we can win the entire city before we can win back a brother who is offended. A lot of it is the Church's fault because we're shouting about salvation, but we don't take the time to say, "You need more than just salvation; you need a time of growth.

You need a time for God to get in you. There are some areas of your life that will need to change."

Growth is Essential

Did you know that if a person is possessed of the devil and believers come together and cast that evil spirit out, the Word says that spirit will come back to see if there is a void (Matt. 12:43–45). If that person the demon was prayed out of hasn't gotten into the Word and filled that void, then that demon comes back with seven more demons and fills—refills—that temple. If the enemy can't drag you back, he'll try to push you overboard.

When you're delivered of what the devil wants to do in your life, when God sets you free from sin, that devil is going to come back to see where you stand. And if you're just banking on that prayer you prayed, you will soon fall. We need Christ in us. We must feed what He birthed in us, or we will die spiritually. Nothing grows without being fed. If you don't feed a baby, it dies. If you don't water and fertilize a garden, it dies.

It's time for God's people to get together and hold their peace—instead of speaking. We need to say, "Father, I know you saved me from sin, but now I need to grow a bit." The Bible says, "But grow in grace, and in the knowledge of our Lord and Savior, Jesus Christ. To him be glory both now and forever" (2 Pet. 3:18). Every created thing seems to have within it the principle of growth. A tree grows from a seed. The birds, fish, and beasts of the field all come to maturity by growth. The human body grows from feeblest infancy into the strength of manhood. The mind grows as well as the body.

Grace Produces Devotion

The grace of God towards men produces devotion. The grace He bestowed upon my life makes me want to be devoted to Him.

We can learn a lot from the old-time saints. Ask some of them, "What did you find in Christ? What has made you hold on for sixty years? I've watched you lose loved ones and seen your finances go bad. I've watched your house burn to the ground, your family walk out on you, and sickness invade your home. What has caused you to hold on?" If you ask them, you will find out it is about more than birth. Birth is just the beginning.

When our baby girl was three or four days old, I got her out of bed so her mama could get some rest. The baby was hungry, so I got out about seven ounces of milk and fed that baby the whole thing. Before I knew it, she threw it all up and started screaming. Her mama came running and demanded "What are you doing to that baby?"

"I'm just trying to help so you can sleep," I said. My intentions were good, but I tried to feed that baby too much too soon.

Too Much Too Soon

Sometimes we try to feed new Christians too much too soon. Someone asked me why I sometimes spend four or five months preaching on the same subject. Because we need a little bit at a time so we can grow.

If you don't give a person time to develop, you can easily harm them. You can't run a ten-mile marathon before you can walk half a mile. Have you ever noticed that when folks get good and fed up with their physical condition, they go out and try to run ten miles? When the ambulance brings them home they say, "Well, I guess it's not God's will for me to exercise." It makes me want to shake them and say, "No, dummy. You need to be able to walk to the mailbox and back before you try to run around the block."

We have to learn to grow gradually. We need to say, "Lord, feed me enough." Someone called me recently and said, "Pastor, I want you to know I've been chewing on what you said last Sunday." I was glad because I have been doing a whole lot of chewing myself lately. I have been getting into the Word and finding out what God is trying to say. God isn't interested in completing a subject overnight—He wants it to get into your spirit. He wants to make you a person that makes a difference in this world

We cannot make a difference until we grow. And we can't grow until we allow the seed to be planted. The planted seed is my decision to serve Christ. I'm something new, and I'm beginning to sprout up. If I humble myself and let the ministry of God feed me, soon there will be a bloom on my life. Soon I'll be like that little candle you can't hide underneath a bushel basket. Pretty soon the community is going to realize there is something different about that guy. "I see a glow about him," they'll say. "He still has the same old ugly body, but there is something different about his appearance." Will they say that because I'll be all grown up? No, I don't think so. The Bible says we will always keep learning and growing because there is always something else we need to know.

I don't care if you've been in the Word for fifty years, God has a brand new chapter for you. He has something else He wants to teach you. Have you ever looked at a Scripture and received from it only to return to it in three or four months and see something completely new and different in it? That is because God, in His infinite wisdom, knows that our minds cannot contain all He has for us at one time.

Prepare the Soil

I have to put myself in a place where I can grow. Churches are ministries that have been planted; they are places where believers come to grow. When we started our church, we dug a hole and threw seed in the ground. For a period of time, we didn't know if there would be a ministry here or not. Now we know that when services are scheduled, someone is going to show up.

It's like a convenience store. When you need a loaf of bread, you don't wonder if the store is still going to be in the same place. You know it is going to be there. When you go to church, you know it will be there.

You may have fussed and carried on like a bunch of heathens on the way to church and then put on a big, old smile when you pulled into the parking lot. We are all guilty of putting on good little fronts. We put on a happy face so everyone will think things are right in our hearts. It is time to accept that something has been birthed in our lives and God is trying to help us grow. But it takes time.

Some of you have already been on good, solid meat for a long time, but many of us are still on milk. Paul told the Corinthians that he had been giving them milk, not meat, because they were not ready for the meat (see 1 Cor. 3:2). There comes a time when you have had enough milk and it's time for something different. When we as believers come together and humble ourselves and say, "OK, God, make out of me what you can make out of me and grow me up in the Lord," then He puts a bloom on our lives.

After a watermelon seed sprouts up and blooms, somewhere around 120 or 130 days later—if the weather is just right—you get watermelons from that vine. You don't plant a watermelon seed and get an onion. You get a watermelon. We are all hooked up to the vine. In John 15:5 Jesus said that He was the vine, and we are the branches. God is doing something in us. He is changing us, growing us, and making us into something for the work.

It's not that we're such a special people but that God has a special calling for us. And therefore, it's going to take special folks to say, "God, I'm willing for you to take me back. Let birth begin again. And Lord, after you've birthed me again and rocked me in the cradle again, begin to grow me up."

I'm trying to help my children grow in the Lord. I am trying to grow my family in the Lord. I'm trying to get the people of God not to be of a fleshly or natural mind but to be of a spiritual mind. Anybody can be spiritual on the mountaintop. We must understand that when we are down in the valley, that is the time for believers to shine.

The friend of a man who won the lottery said, "I'm not going to work anymore because my friend won a lot of money, and he's going to take care of me." That may work with lottery winnings, but it doesn't work spiritually. No one can give you his growth and maturity. You have to grow in Christ yourself.

Process, not Product

You can't be in Christ without growing. Being in Christ is all *about* growing. It means I am going to grow up and respond differently next year than I did this year. Ask the Lord, "Just grow me up in you." When I'm devoted to Christ, it's because of God's grace. His grace is why He died on the cross. His grace is why we grow up in Him. When we are tired and worn, His grace is alive. It is time to get in the Word and grow. To grow in grace, is to grow in virtue. It is to grow in faith. It is to grow in meekness. It is to grow in gentleness. It means you stop being an old know-it-all.

It is one thing to grab a product. But growth is not a product; it is a process. We have to get into the Bible and allow the baby to be born. Then Christ will begin to instill meekness, humbleness, and a spirit of forgiveness. Today, I would rather forgive a person than to fight them. A few years ago, I would have rather fought than forgiven.

Meekness. Humbleness. Virtue. Grace. Love one for the other. In this growth of right principles, the old principles will begin to weaken and decay. The change is so gradual, you won't even realize it at first. It is like a newborn baby. It seems like only a few days after birth that the child is crawling. And then before you know it, the baby is walking.

It is the same with spiritual birth. We give our lives, then we begin to change. Sometimes you don't recognize the change until someone tries to run you off the road. Three months earlier you would have given them a piece of your mind, but now you notice that you prayed, "Lord, protect that nut." While God is instilling His virtue, meekness, love, and grace in you, He is taking away the bad attitudes and selfishness. You will find yourself caring about people you used to hate.

When we started this church, there were some preachers I couldn't stand. Recently, I met up with one of them at a restaurant. He walked in, and it didn't bother me a bit. When I got in the car my wife said, "Well, how do you feel?" When I said that I felt great, she asked, "You mean it didn't bother you to see that man?" That is when I saw the evidence of God working in my life. He had changed my heart.

Ask God to touch your heart. Get in the Word every day. If you are still a baby believer, then go to the Word and be fed on the milk. If you've been in the milk long enough, then dig deeper and start chewing on some meat. Growth takes time, but it won't happen if you are not willing to give God control. We all need Him to feed us and grow us. Next time you go to church, tell God you didn't come for a quick fix but to receive the Word, a piece of bread you can take with you and allow to work in your spirit. Tell Him the areas you need Him to deal with.

The Father will rock you in His arms and feed you like a little baby. He will keep feeding you and keep feeding you. Ask Him to take over the areas in your life that are out of control. He will touch them and break the bondage. He will send His love and grace in a mighty way. Only by His grace can we be *in* Christ, not merely *of* Christ. He will give us joy in the valley times—not just when everything is going well.

Are you tired of milk? Then ask Him for steak.

Chapter Seven

Meekness is not Weakness

I have settled in my life that no matter what I face, God has already faced it. No matter what tomorrow holds for my life, God has already held that day in His hand. In 2 Peters 3:9 it says He is not slack concerning His Word. If He has planned a future for my life, then He has already walked that life for me. There are no surprises in what I will face tomorrow. And what I face today is simply an opportunity to know God in a brand new way.

Many believers miss this because they come to the place of salvation and say, "I've found everything in Christ." No, you found a decision, a beginning. Now it is time to know more about the one you decided to serve. When I got married, I decided to live with this woman, but now I will spend the rest of my life getting to know the one I decided to live with. Our marriage to Christ is the same way. You accept Christ and marry yourself to Him as He married himself to you. Then you begin to learn more about the one you married. Marriage is the foundation. You don't go out into the desert, plant a seed, and say, "I hope it grows." You try to find good, fertile soil. You work the ground and get to know the ground. Like a good farmer knows his ground, a good strong Christian knows the Savior. There will come a trial or temptation—if it hasn't already—when we will need to know the Christ we decided to serve. We will need to call on Him and say, "Lord, I trusted you. Now I need to see your Word."

Something is Brewing

Isn't God a good God? I am happy with my God. The day I allowed myself to be satisfied in Him, I found a peace in spite of circumstances. Whether I stand or fall in this life, I know where I am going to spend eternity. If I wake up with a headache or backache, with a dollar in my pocket or nothing in my pocket, I know I am going to be OK because something on the inside is brewing. Something is happening. Have you ever smelled that good old pot of coffee brewing? You can't get at it just yet, but you know that in just a few minutes it's going to be something. The Lord has been busy cooking us a big old pot of coffee.

People like to talk, and often we like to look around and find somebody we can pick on. Denominations criticize other denominations that don't do it the way they do. Some of us have looked at Baptists and said, "Ah, they are just a bunch of dead beats." But when we look closer we have to say, "Boy, don't they know the Word." They know whom they serve, and they know why they serve Him. When they stand in the community to make a statement, they can say it with vigor and strength and authority because they have an understanding.

I am proud to have been raised in the Pentecostal movement, but I feel we missed some things. There are a few things I believe I would teach my children differently. I would teach them that to serve Christ they need to know about this person they serve. I would teach them that if they are going to attend a church, then they need to learn about that ministry. Don't just go in and be satisfied with what you see on the surface. What is the direction and motive of the ministry? Why are you there, and why are they there? Are there any miracles? Does anyone find Christ? Are the people better off this week than they were last week? Why does that church exist?

We have spent a lot of time on 2 Corinthians 5:17, looking at the characteristics of true Christianity. A true Christian knows the character of the person in whom they believe. It is not enough in the latter times to give lip service. The lip service days are over. It is time to get down to reality. It is time to get into the Word and say, "Lord, teach me how I can truly be in you." I don't know about you, but I find myself continuously walking through valleys that I can't share with someone else. I have to know enough of the Word and have enough of God—this God I say I serve—in my spirit that He and I can work it out.

Changing Tracks

We can't just take our Bibles and say, "I know this is God's Word, and as long as I have it with me, I'm protected." No, if you don't read it, it is no different from a comic book. You have to get in this book. You have to know that birth comes through faith. Faith operates through obedience. And faith without works is dead (James 2:26). When one has been born again, as the Word speaks of that new birth, his principles and motives, his aims, and his habits all change. All things become new. Suddenly, instead of wanting to curse you, I want to bless you. Instead of wanting to be poor little pitiful me, I want to praise God and say, "Look what He has worked in my life." Instead of coming into the house of God to see what I can take, I come to the house of God to see what I can give. The motive changes.

Take, for example, a steam locomotive. It may change course, but every rod, axle, and wheel still works the same way—it's just moving in a new direction. Just like believers. I was headed this way, but praise God, now I'm going that way. I was headed for death and sin, but now I'm headed in a whole new direction. Paul was headed to Damascus to destroy God's people when suddenly he changed directions.

The whole tenure and direction of our lives have to change when new birth comes. I have had people say, "Praise God, Pastor, my tenure in life has changed, and I'm a different person now. I'm a new creature in Christ so why don't you get off this subject and teach me something else?" Because birth is not enough. We need to take time to grow. A mother cannot give birth to a child and then lay it in a crib and say, "I'll see you in eighteen years." That mother has to feed, nourish, and love that child. That child knows immediately, even before hunger, if it's loved or not.

We have to grow up in Christ. A person who doesn't mean to grow doesn't grow. That is why we have thirty-year babies. There are folks who have been sitting in the house of God week in and week out for thirty years, but they don't know a bit more about the Word today than they did thirty years ago.

We get so caught up in what the preacher, or the preacher's wife, or the neighbor is doing that we never make an attempt to grow spiritually. I have had people meet me at the door after the Sunday sermon and say, "Pastor, I sure hope those people were listening this morning." I want to grab my little microphone and yell, "You were the one I was talking to." But I can't straighten your life out until I straighten my life out. Matthew 7:3 asks how can I get that itty-bitty splinter out of your eye when there's a big old beam hanging in my own eye? There comes a time when I have to grow up in Christ. There comes a time when, even though you hurt me, I am able to survive without holding a grudge.

Elements of Grace

The Word says in 2 Peter 3:18, "But grow in grace and in the knowledge of our Lord and Savior, Jesus Christ. To him be glory both now and for ever." We know that every created thing has within it the principle of growth. If I'm going to grow in grace, my love of God is going to have to grow. I am going to have to know more about Him. I can't just be satisfied with what the preacher told me. I'm going to have to get in the good Book and walk through some trials and tribulations to find out for myself who God is.

In order to grow in grace, we must know the ingredients for growth. To grow in grace, we must grow in virtue, faith, meekness, gentleness, patience, a spirit of forgiveness, and usefulness.

The Lord began to deal with me about this area and I said, "Lord, I've already told the people this is what they need to grow."

He said, *"But what good does it do for you to tell them they need to grow in virtue if they don't know what virtue is? What good is it to tell them to grow in faith if they don't know what faith is? Or meekness? Or gentleness? Or patience? Or the spirit of forgiveness? Or usefulness?"*

Some of us have to back up about forty years and say, "God, if grace is the main ingredient for me to grow in Christ, then teach me about grace."

He says, *"OK, let's look at virtue."*

The Value of Virtue

Virtue is moral excellence or goodness. Philippians 4:8 says "Finally, brethren, whatsoever things are true, whatsoever things are honest, whatsoever things are just, whatsoever things are pure, whatsoever things are lovely, whatsoever things are of good report; if there be any virtue and if there be any praise, think on these things."

Moral excellence. That means when you go somewhere, you're about goodness. People can see that you are a good moral person. That's a person of virtue. If I'm going to grow in grace, I can't go around hurting everyone in my path and saying, "I'm a godly person because I'm in His grace." I have to have a moral strength.

Virtue is a necessary ingredient in the exercise of faith. In 2 Peter 1:3 we are told, "According as his divine power hath given unto us all things that pertain unto life and godliness, through the knowledge of him that hath called us to glory and virtue." Verse 5 says, "And besides this, giving all diligence, add to your faith virtue; and to virtue knowledge."

Add virtue. There is the seed of being faithful, but I have to add virtue. I add to that by upholding morals. I pity the believer who has to go around saying, "I'm a believer." I would rather see it on his face. I would rather you see something about my life I don't have to tell you about. I just want to know about Jesus. In 1 Corinthians 2:2 (paraphrase) Paul says, "I choose to know nothing of you." You don't need to know how I mow my lawn. You just need to know about Jesus in my life. That's our concern here. Our concern is not who lives on the east or west side. The concern here is who can get in Christ, who can be a virtuous person, who can grow in grace.

I want to talk just for a moment about another side of virtue. The Greek word for virtue often comes across as a word of power. In Luke 8:45–46, Jesus asked, "Who touched me?" The disciples answered that a whole bunch of people were touching Him. He clarified that somebody had touched Him, and He perceived that virtue had left His body. When you are a person of grace and mercy and virtue, then just by the way you shake someone's hand, virtue can flow and heal that person's body. I can't tell you about the times someone has hugged me and never said a word, but the grip and the virtue said it all. If you really want to touch someone, walk up, put a grip on him, and let God flow from you to him. God will begin to cleanse you and wash you out. That's another side of virtue.

Faith Follows

Not only do we have to grow in virtue but also we must have faith. Faith is a confident attitude toward God, involving commitment to His will of one's life. Are you confident in God? If you say, "I live by faith, but I'm just not sure if God can take me through this one," then you're not confident. You can't grow in His grace until you are confident that if you put your last ten dollars in the offering, God will provide food for your family to eat next week. Faith says I may starve to death, but I'm going to give what rightfully belongs to God. I cannot grow in grace until I grow in faith. Faith makes me work. Faith makes me do something about what I have been taught. Faith makes me get up and make my home a better place to live. Put some paint on that old barn and make it look like something. If you drive an old beat up car, wash that thing and treat it like it's a limousine. The Bible says when you have done all you can do, stand up and hold on because a miracle's coming your way. When I have done all I can do with what God has entrusted to me, when I've allowed my faith to go as far as I know about faith, He will give me more faith.

Hebrews 11:1–2 says, "Now faith is the substance of things hoped for, and the evidence of things not seen. For by it, the elders obtained a good report." Having faith expresses God's grace operating in your life. The Church has fallen too soon, too quick, and for too long for every scam and story that comes along. We are to be people of integrity. We should be people who know the difference. We should be people who speak the truth instead of receiving everything that comes through the door. That's what destroys the body of Christ. We have to be people of faith.

The Meaning of *Meekness*

As I was studying grace, I said, "OK, God, I can share about virtue and I can share about having faith, but Lord I don't know a whole lot about meekness." He said, *"Why don't you research it and let's see what we can find?"* See, the Lord always tells you what's wrong and then He says, *"Come now, let's reason together. Let's talk about this thing"* (see Isa. 1:18). I sat down and discovered that meekness is an attitude of humility toward God and gentleness toward people springing from a recognition that God is in control. Whoa. There are a lot of believers running around who don't understand that God is in control. There have been times in my life I have been fearful because I forgot that God was in control.

People with an attitude of humility toward God are humbled that God would save them. Have you met any believers who think that their talents are going to make God look good? Folks, God doesn't need us to make Him look good. God needs us to be a humble people. Not only humble towards Him but also gentle with each other.

Although weakness and meekness may look similar, they are not the same. Weakness is due to negative circumstances such as lack of strength or lack of courage. Meekness is due to a person's conscious choice. Matthew 5:5 says, "Blessed are the meek." Why? Because they inherit the Kingdom of God. We want to inherit something before we have the goods or the formula to inherit. The Apostle Paul once pointed out that the spiritual leaders of the Church have great power, but he cautioned them to refrain themselves in meekness. Galatians 6:1 says, "Brethren, if a man be overtaken in a fault, ye which are spiritual, restore such an one in the spirit of meekness." Galatians 5:22–23 tells us, "But the fruit of the spirit is love, joy, peace, long-suffering, gentleness, goodness, faith, meekness, temperance: against such there is no law." If I'm going to be a humble person towards God and understand that God is in control, then I must treat you with meekness.

I began to think about the old westerns. In them, the cowboy could walk into the bank and get a loan on a handshake. That began to eat at me. We shake hands all the time, every day. *God bless you. Nice to see you again.* But what does that person mean when they shake my hand? Are they wiping something on me I need to see? What does it mean when someone hugs me? If I'm a believer and you're a believer, and if I'm in Christ and you're in Christ, when we shake hands, it should mean something.

Our handshake should say, "Brother, if you're hungry, I'll feed you. If you're naked, I'll clothe you. Sister, in the midnight hour, if you need somebody to pray with you, come knock on my door and I'll be there for you." Meekness means I'm humble towards God and kind and gentle towards my brother. It is high time for men to have a message behind that handshake. If he says, "It was good to see you today," he also means that if my ox gets in the ditch, he'll help me get it out. It's time for the ladies to greet each other with a holy hug and say, "Sister, more than ever before, you need me and I need you, and I'm going be there for you," instead of giving lip service. Why do marriages fail? Because of lip service. Why do churches fail? Because of lip service. Why are there no miracles? Because of lip service.

I told God I want to grow in grace and He said, *"OK, I'm about to take you to school. Learn something about virtue. Learn something about faith. Learn something about meekness."* Meekness is an ingredient. In 2 Corinthians 10:1 Paul said even though he wasn't with them, he would speak with meekness and out of boldness. God's people need to learn how to love each other, not judge each other. The Lord said He wants us to grow in meekness. It's a vital ingredient. To ignore it is like leaving the eggs out of a cake. If any man be in Christ, he's a new creature. It's OK to stand firm, but do it with meekness. Do it out of love. Do it out of compassion.

When the body of Christ has love one for one another, that's revival. When I get totally out of myself, and I say, "God, I'm humbled that you would use me," that's when change comes. God is teaching us how to accept each other. It doesn't matter what your life has been. We accept each other. When God's people grow in grace, they grow in meekness, in faith, in virtue. Through His grace, He molds us together and makes us strong.

Chapter Eight

Stand Firm

God is so good part of the time. Why do I say that? Because we live and act as though God is only good part of the time. The rest of the time we gripe, grumble, and complain. We act as though He is only good part of the time, but He desires to be God in our lives all the time.

The world needs more than lip service. We are learning to let Christ shine. But Christ doesn't shine when we live as if God is only God part of the time. Then it is just words. Our desire should be for God to be God all the time and for Christ to be Christ all the time. The Holy Spirit should be the Holy Spirit in our lives all the time.

To be a Christlike person all the time, we must allow cheerfulness to come. Somebody needs to see that we have someone worth living for, someone worth celebrating. We have something to smile about. I may not be where I need to be, but I'm on my way. I am better off this week than I was last week. I am on the way to sanctification, to becoming a person Christ would be pleased with.

Gentleness, not Judgment

When you're trying to win the lost, yes, you need to be adamant in your belief and firm about your faith, but at the same time, there has to be gentleness in the way you handle people. We don't want to chase them off. We know people are going to go to hell if they don't accept Christ, but there is a way we can be meek in winning the lost. Because of our authority as believers, we so often come across as the great judge, but we are not the judge. We're just sinners saved by God's grace.

As I was thinking about all this, I went to the warehouse one morning and a gentleman walked out of the little storefront and said, "If you go through the gate without an automobile, the gate's not going to open for you to get back out."

I said, "It's no big deal, I'll just shut the power off at the corner of the building."

The man yelled, "You can't touch the power."

I walked on as though it was none of my concern—and it shouldn't have been any of his. After we got inside, I said to my wife, "If that gentleman comes over here and dabbles in my business again, I'm going punch him in the mouth."

She said, "When are you going to begin teaching about meekness and gentleness?"

I thought about that, and it began to work on me.

I said, "Lord, how do we deal with religious folks? Because the Church seems to miss this." We have the attitude that when we are in Christ, we are a gentle calm, that we're pure and righteous. Heaven forbid we say anything out of line or raise our voices. We are to turn the other cheek and praise God, when we turn that cheek, there's another one to turn. And then once we turn that one, there's another one. Christ did not say, "Just be a forgiver and let them treat you like you're a piece of dirt."

I began saying, "Lord, how do you handle the religious ones? How do you handle situations? How am I to be a person of integrity but also a person of meek value?"

The Lord said, *"I want to take you through the Scriptures and show you some things."*

Has anyone ever called you and said, "Did you know the pastor this, or the neighbor that, or this person or the Sunday school teacher did such and such?" Pretty soon your life is filled with listening to the garbage, junk, and filth.

Then when you finally stand up and say, "Don't call me with your junk," the whole group gets offended.

They say, "Well, he's not a man of God. He told us to be of meek value. He wears the name of one thing, but he's acting like something else. It's not religious. It's not the way I've been trained. He's not as kind as he used to be."

Examples to Follow

It's one thing to handle a sinner. But then there are folks who know just enough Scripture to keep the whole multitude in a big mess in the name of God. I said, "Lord, we're supposed to be humble and meek, so how am I supposed to respond?"

He said, *"Do you remember my Son, Christ?"*

I said, "Well yeah. I teach about him every week."

He said, *"Do you remember when He went into the temple? What did He do?"*

I said, "He kicked the tables over. He got in their face. He told them, 'You made my father's house a den of thieves. You're making a mockery of this place. This temple is to be a house of prayer'" (Matt. 21:12–13, paraphrased).

Jesus was still meek, humble, and loving, but He was emphatic. His message was: "You're tearing my father's house apart, and I'm not going to tolerate it."

When God met Moses out in the field in the form of a burning bush, He said essentially, "I want you to do something for me. I've heard the cries of my children, and I need someone to go set them free. I chose you to go" (see Exod. 3).

That's quite an honor. But Moses said, "Lord, who—who am I to save them? Isn't there someone else you can use? And how will they know I'm from you?" (Exodus 3:11–13, paraphrased)

Then God told Moses to throw the stick in his hand on the ground, and the stick became a hissing snake. Then God told Moses to pick it up by the tail, and the snake became a rod again (Exod. 4:3–4). God used that stick to show Moses that he had the power and the anointing. God said, "I'll fill your mouth in the time that you need something to say. I'll give you the words, and I'll help you respond. They'll know you're from me." (Exodus 4:11, paraphrased)

Moses then reminded the Lord that he did not speak well.

The Word says that God was angry. Moses was equipped because God called him, yet all Moses gave were excuses until finally the Lord got angry. Moses knew God. He knew the Word, and he knew the one who had called him. But the anger of the Lord had to deal with him. God had to set him straight.

I said, "OK, Lord, so you're saying it's OK to have a little bit of authority. You're saying that maybe sometimes we should stop holding hands. OK, Lord, you've shown me enough."

The Lord said to me, "*No, I haven't. Don't you remember Saul in the Book of Acts? He was on the road to Damascus to destroy, and I had to go and meet him. 'Saul. Saul. Why do you persecute me?' Do you think I just walked up with a picnic basket and said, "Hey buddy, why are you messing with me?"*

God spoke to Paul in such an emphatic voice that it changed his whole mind and tenure in life. Paul simply asked, "What must I do?" (Acts 9:6, paraphrased)

I said, "OK, Lord, now I understand."

God said, "*No, you don't. Look in Luke, chapter 10. I sent the seventy out to minister and witness and perform miracles, and when they came back, what was the report?*"

Can you believe that the devils are subjects to us? Can you believe it? Christ said, "You shouldn't be so surprised that my word is truth." He says, "But you are to be celebrating because your name is written." (Luke 10:17–20, paraphrased) He had to deal with them.

I said, "Lord, now I understand."

God said, "*No, you don't. Look in Matthew 16:18. Peter was asked questions and gave the right answers, and Christ said, '…thou art Peter, and upon this rock I will build my church; and the gates of hell shall not prevail against it.'*"

A couple of verses later, where Christ begins to share what will happen in his own life, Peter, out of nowhere, says, "No." He rebuked Christ. Can I say to you that when you rebuke a man of God, you rebuke Christ? When you rebuke your Sunday school teacher, your worship leader, or things going on in the name of the Most High, you are rebuking Christ. What did Christ say to His good buddy, Peter? "Oh, it's OK man. Come on, let's go have a hamburger. Come on Peter, tell me what you're feeling. Let's gossip for a while." No. He basically said, "Peter, shut up. You're letting the devil speak through you, for you savor not the things of God, but the things of man" (see Matt. 16: 23).

I said, "God, what are you saying?"

He replied, "*Son, there comes a time when believers have to stand up and be believers. There comes a time when you can only take so much junk.*"

The evening after Christ's conversation with Peter, Christ rode a little borrowed colt into the city. He was tired, beaten, and worn. He went to the temple and saw what was happening, and afterwards, the Word says, He left. He just left. He walked in and they ignored Him. He left, ate, rested. I believe He cried. I believe He cried all through the night because He knew what He would have to do. He cried for people He loved. They were not ignorant. They were religious people who knew better.

An unsaved person is ignorant of the things of God and needs to learn, and we need to show love. But these people knew better. The next day, He went back to the temple. When He walked through the door, everybody knew Jesus was in the house. He kicked tables. He let them know real quick, "My house shall be called the house of prayer" (Matt. 21: 13). He was so emphatic it shook the entire temple. They said the sick came in and He began to heal them. From damnation to blessing, just that quick is God's grace.

Stand for Your Faith

Being people of meek value means we love, teach, and nourish sinners. But because we call ourselves believers, we also stand up for what we believe—because we know better.

I said, "OK, God, that's what you're saying. I wish I had known this a few months ago because I wanted to speak my mind a few times." Right about that time, I received one of those phone calls from an unhappy former church member. This person had resigned by letter and was now spreading stories to the other church members.

After talking a few minutes he asked, "Do you feel I was wrong in my letter?"

I said, "Yeah, you were. You shared with me how you felt left out, but what about the day I spent over two hundred dollars at Outback Steakhouse with three different families? Your family was one of them. What about the night at Red Lobster when I picked up the tab? What about all those times you were at my home for fellowship? I included you. What about the new set of tires I bought for you and the rent I paid? What about the night I approached you and asked if you were OK? You lied and told me you were fine. I went through a year and a half of that with you."

When I got off the phone, my wife asked, "Well, what did he say?"

I said, "Well, for the last twenty minutes, he didn't say a thing."

What am I saying? I'm saying as believers, as people who are growing, we have to learn to stand up for what we believe in. You don't have to be ugly, mean, or nasty, and you don't have to punch someone in the mouth, but you can punch spiritually.

There comes a time that as a child of God, I have the right to defend my beliefs. When someone comes against what I've given my life for, I have a right to stand and fight—and so do you. You might say I was mean to that person, but when you slap me in the face, you are slapping the entire congregation. Don't think you're going to tear me down and remain friends.

To grow in meekness and the grace of God, we must know how to handle the dear one who needs Christ as Savior. We need to show them the love of the Lord, but at the same time, 1 Peter 5:8 says, "Be sober, be vigilant."

Look at Peter. One moment he had the character of God because he spoke the words of God. Christ said that upon the rock of Peter surely He would build His church. And not only would He build it but also the gates of hell could not prevail against that house. Just a few minutes later, Peter found he couldn't bear the thought of losing his friend, so he rebuked Christ. He didn't take time to understand that it was expedient for Christ to go away and that if He went away, the comforter, the Holy Ghost, would come.

Just as Peter didn't want his friend to suffer, I don't want my ministry to go through trials, either. But if it will raise us up to be Christlike, then let's walk through the valley. If any man be in Christ, he's a new creature. He's not an old grump. He's changed. He's committed. He's a person of integrity. We say, "This hurts and it's painful, and I don't quite understand it, but I stand."

If your phone rings with the garbage, you can put a stop to it. Stand your ground. I felt peace come over my life when I hung up that phone. Not because I had an opportunity to tell someone off. That part hurts. I still love those people, but I hate their ways. I will no longer stand still while people take out of my pocket and spit in my face.

There are too many examples in the Word of the anger of the Lord. He still used Moses, but He had to talk straight to him. He still used Samson. Samson was on his way to marry a heathen when he faced a young lion and the spirit of the Lord come upon him. Even in his rebellion, the spirit of the Lord came upon him. Sometimes, when that lion comes at you, you have to stand up and say, "Father, give me the words." Then speak the word and go on.

Romans 11:29 tells us the gifts and calling of God are without repentance. He called you for such a time as this. He has anointed you. He set you free that you may set others free. He built you up that you may build others up, but sometimes you have to tear them down to build them up. Haven't you ever been knocked down and when you got up, you were a better person? If any man be in Christ, he is a new creature. No more old things.

Don't be a weak-kneed believer. If He gave His life (and you know He did), and if He saved you (and you know He did), don't let anyone steal that from you. If God called you to be part of a ministry, stand and go boldly to the throne room. Say, "Father inasmuch as I know that I am under extreme attack, I know that I'm victorious. I may look like I'm beaten. I may look like I'm in the valley, but on the inside there's a war going on and there's a fire of the Holy Ghost beginning to burn. I may not feel like getting out of bed or standing my ground, but the spirit of God is about to rise up and show me the light."

By His faith you were saved. It was His Son's blood that was shed. Not your blood, but His blood. His message to us is: "If you would accept by faith through obedience, I'll give you a new birth. You'll be a new creature and I'll raise you up. I'll show you my word living out in your life." It's one thing for the Word to be in the book. It's another thing for the Word to be lived out.

When will we allow Christ to make us new creatures? Beloved, if you don't learn to fight for your family, you're going to lose them. If you don't learn to fight for your ministry, you're going lose it. If you don't learn to fight for brothers and sisters and mamas and daddies, you're going lose them. How do I fight? With meekness. Go to your prayer pose and say, "Father, how do I handle this?" And sometimes He's going say, *"You handle it with a tear,"* and other times He's going say, *"Walk in and kick the tables over and let them know you've had enough and you're not taking it anymore."*

It's time for God's people to stand up and be strong for what they believe. It's time to quit worrying about the past, but that doesn't mean I'm taking a back seat. He saved me and healed me of leukemia. He kept my broken home together and healed my broken heart. He healed my child of chemical burns and took me places I could have never gone. I'm not taking a back seat.

If you would put the word *commitment* as a focus in your life, the confusion would go away. God still is waiting on you to make a decision. He wants to be the Christ that you live for and not the Christ of the world. He'll give your searching heart rest if you'll allow commitment to come. He committed His Son's life. His Son—who at any moment could have said He'd had enough—said in essence, "I'm committed. I'm going to the cross, and they are going to take my life. But I'm going to conquer death and hell, and I'm going to rise up and ascend to the right hand of the Father."

He was committed to the end. He expects no less from us.

Chapter Nine

Smile—and Shut Up

We often get so wrapped up in trying to please everyone else, we forget that our responsibility is to be in Christ. Joshua 24:15 says, "Choose you this day whom ye will serve." Whom are you serving? I am going to serve Him.

You can't walk out on God. You cannot deny Christ and expect to have peace in this life. Neither can you go through life supposing you know Christ, only to find you have simply been holding on to Christ. If any man be in Christ, it's different from holding on to Christ.

The Lord is teaching us. We have learned about being born into Christ. Some of us were born into junk, and some of us have been infiltrated with junk for many, many years. If it doesn't bring us closer to Christ, it must be junk.

A young lady asked her mother if she could go to the movies. She told her mother the movie was rated R but that it was a good, fun movie, and would be real exciting. While she was talking, her mother was making a tossed salad. After she put in the tomatoes, cucumbers, lettuce, and onions, the mother suddenly reached into the garbage can and scooped up a handful of trash and old food. She cut it up and put it in the salad.

The young lady said, "Momma, what are you doing? Have you lost your mind?"

The mother said, "You know the old saying, 'garbage in, garbage out.' If you want to go see garbage, you may as well eat garbage, too."

We need to understand what garbage is and what it isn't. The Word of God is not garbage. The Word of God wants to teach us and instruct us. He said "If any man be in Christ." There needs to be a new birth. After that birth comes a period of growth—and that period lasts a lifetime. You should never stop growing in Christ.

Know What Came Before—and What's Ahead

In 2 Peter 3:1 it says, "Beloved, I now write unto you; in both which I stir up your pure minds by way of remembrance." Sometimes we need to hear things we've already heard. I can remember times my daddy whooped me, and before long, he'd have to whoop me again. He was reminding me that Daddy was Daddy. Do you know that the Father is the Father? And the Word is the Word? It's OK for somebody to stir you up and help you remember things you were taught in the past.

> That ye may be mindful of the words which were spoken before by the holy prophets, and of the commandment of us the apostles of the Lord and Savior: Knowing this first, that there shall come in the last days scoffers, walking after their own lusts, and say-

ing, Where is the promise of his coming? for since the fathers fell asleep, all things continue as they were from the beginning of the creation...But, beloved, be not ignorant of this one thing, that one day is with the Lord as a thousand years, and a thousand years as one day. The Lord is not slack concerning His promise, as some men count slackness; but is long-suffering to us-ward, not willing that any should perish, but that all should come to repentance. But the day of the Lord will come as a thief in the night; in the which the heavens shall pass away with a great noise, and the elements shall melt with fervent heat, the earth also and the works that are therein shall be burned up. Seeing then that all these things shall be dissolved, what manner of persons ought ye to be.... (2 Pet. 3:2–4, 8–11a)

What kind of person should you be? If you know the world's coming to an end and the Lord's going to return, and if you accept the Word of truth, then what kind of person should you be? In 2 Peter 3:11b it says, "In all holy conversation and godliness." That would leave out about 90% of those who call themselves *believers*, because I'm not sure there is a group anywhere which talks only about the positive and about holiness and righteousness. Is there a people anywhere who look at God for the goodness of God, instead of making a mockery of God? People tell me I shouldn't say things like that. It's OK. It's my place to tell the truth—and the truth is we should be a people of holy conversation. We should be people without murmuring and complaining. We should be people who would take a stand and be the righteousness of God.

Verses 12–15a say:

Looking for and hastening unto the coming of the day of God, wherein the heavens being on fire shall be dissolved, and the elements shall melt with fervent heat? Nevertheless we, according to His promise, look for new heavens and a new earth, wherein dwelleth righteousness. Wherefore beloved, seeing that ye look for such things, be diligent that ye may be found of him in peace, without spot, and blameless. And account that the long-suffering of our Lord is salvation.

Some people think because the Lord is long-suffering, they can live like a heathen and get away with it. But my Bible tells me I have no promise of tomorrow. And we're nothing more than heathens when we play games with God. We come in on Sunday and praise God. But on Monday, we don't want anything to do with God.

And account that the long-suffering of our Lord is salvation; even as our beloved brother Paul also according to the wisdom given unto him hath written unto you; As also in all his epistles, speaking in them of these things; in which are some things hard to be understood.... (vv. 15b–16a)

That means it's good to come into the house of God to be taught. It's good to get into the Word and say "Lord, what are you saying here?" It's good to look at the circumstances, the situation you're having to deal with in life, and say, "Lord, what meaneth this?"

Growing up, I asked my father many questions. God is God and we are His little children. That lets us know we can question our heavenly Father, not with a bad attitude, but to say, "Lord, what do you mean by that? Lord, why am I walking through this valley, and what do you want me to gain out of it? I don't want to go through this again, Lord. I've had enough of this pain. Teach me so that I can go on to something else." Have you ever been there? Found things in Scripture that are hard to understand? Be very careful that you don't look at a scripture on the surface, say you know what it means, and then pervert it and change it into what you want it to be. In other words, don't use Scripture to make yourself feel good about sin.

Verse 17 says, "Ye therefore, beloved, seeing ye know these things before, beware lest ye also, being led away with the error of the wicked, fall from your own steadfastness." He's saying, "Listen, some of you know this. Some of you understand this thing, and some of you understand how you are supposed to live. But listen, there are some slick folks out there. There are some folks that are so good at perverting Scripture. Be careful or you will slip away from your steadfastness."

That is why 2 Corinthians 6:14 warns us against being unequally yoked together with unbelievers. You should be able to discern who you are around. Be careful, lest you lose your steadfastness. Notice here what He says in the final verse of the chapter. After he's told us all of these things, he said, "But grow in grace" (v. 18). That tells me that just because I've been in it for forty years, I still need to grow.

There is something else about God that I have missed—I need to know more of Him. If I'm going to understand the characteristics of a true Christian, then every day I need something brand new. Everyday I need to be able to take off the old and say, "Lord, put in the new. Lord, teach me." He said, "But grow in grace and in the knowledge of our Lord and Savior, Christ Jesus. To him be glory both now and forever" (v. 18).

We've been taking the word *grace* and saying, "OK Lord, if grace is what we are to grow in, then teach us the elements that are in grace." What is the character of grace? We know that in grace there is virtue. We've talked about meekness. Paul said that we have authority; we even have leverage with the folks. But with a sinner, we are to refrain ourselves in meekness. Be firm, be adamant, but show much love in winning that sinner to Christ.

Then Paul began to teach us about the other side of meekness and how to handle religious folks. I submit to you that religious folks are different from Christians. Take a minute or two to take that one in. Religious folks are different from Christians. Religious folks are of Christ. Some are so heavenly bound they are no earthly good. They know the Word. Boy, they can tell you the Word, but then they go out and live something else. They say one thing, but then they do another.

If we just sit for weeks and weeks, or even years and years, and learn how to be in Christ, but we don't receive it, then it will produce unrest. We must be a people of a sound mind. I know where I'm going, and I know who called me. He has not given me a spirit of cowardice, but He gave me the spirit through the power of the Holy Ghost that I may stand and be a person of tenure. A person of virtue. A person of faith. A person of meekness.

After I studied meekness, I said, "OK, Lord, we know about meekness. What are the other ingredients we need to talk about?"

And the Lord said, "*You need to know something about gentleness.*" So I studied gentleness. The Apostle Paul declared Christians should have a spirit of gentleness toward all people. Look at Philippians 4:5: "Let your moderation be known unto all men." Why? "The Lord is at hand."

Rejoice Anyway

Notice what Paul said in Philippians 4:4. "Rejoice in the Lord always." We read that as rejoice in the Lord when we feel like it. Rejoice in the Lord when there are other believers around. Rejoice in the Lord when everything is going great. The Word said rejoice in the Lord always. Every day, every minute, every moment. Every day of your life, find something to rejoice about. "Pastor, it's really bad right now." But look how good it is. The glass is not half empty, it's half full. Rejoice in the Lord.

I asked, "Lord, how do I teach the people about rejoicing?"

He said, *"There are some elements of the Christian character the people need to understand."*

I want to talk about three elements that will change your life and let your neighbor know where you stand. First of all, we are going to talk about cheerfulness. There isn't anything worse than a bunch of grumpy believers. There is nothing worse than believers who walk through the door with their heads dragging in the mud and then leave with them dragging in the sand. There isn't anything worse. I'm just telling you the truth of the matter. Churches in America want people to come in and be part of God's kingdom, but we are the most sour-looking folks on the face of the earth.

If the Philippians neglected or undervalued this duty, they had many imitators. Some professing Christians set their face against cheerfulness and make the best of days into the saddest. They'll make the best of books seem most forbidding. The best of services, the least inviting. There are those who take their cues from this and come to regard sourness and holiness as synonymous. They become so heavenly bound, they never take time to deal with the issues at hand, always looking so far beyond that they miss the point. We act as if we have all the answers, but we don't even know all the questions. This is a gross perversion of living for God.

The Bible is a book of education. Why are some things hard for me to understand? Because He wants me to be educated. I can read some scriptures and know what He is saying. Then there are other scriptures that take a period of time for me to understand. That's how we mature. You don't take a sixth-grader and teach him twelfth-grade material. It is the same with living for God. He teaches us a bit at a time as we mature spiritually. You may say, "I just don't feel that I'm maturing." Have you been in the Book lately?

We degrade the service of God and Christianity when we get so hooked on what we should be that we forget whom we should rejoice in. We are to rejoice in the Lord. So rejoice in the Lord always. That means I get my mind and heart off you and quit worrying about my present valley and the mud hole I'm in. Instead, I say, "Lord, I see you out there, and I know you're about to come back for me. I've got something to be cheerful about."

We are believers, but there is no cheerfulness. If any man be in Christ, he's a brand new creature. We have something to be cheerful about. We're not old grumps if we are truly in Christ. One can be an old grump at fifteen years of age, so don't get down on folks who are a little more seasoned. I'm not speaking of age, but some of us—at fifteen years old—think we know more than God himself. All that does is breed disruption and disappointment in our lives and ultimately, we become blamers of God. We would avoid about 90% of the troubles in our churches if the people would stick together and be cheerful.

When it looks foggy and I can't see past my feet, I know God is at hand. I know that He is coming soon. I know there is something to celebrate. *Lord, I don't know how we're going to get to the other side, but I feel you tugging at the rope.*

We must practice putting smiles on our faces. I'm not the best at it, but the Lord is working on me. There's a smile in my heart, and it was not birthed by people. It was birthed by the one who forgave me of sin and picked me up for the nine hundredth time and gave me hope. He gave me something to be cheerful about. Philippians 4:4 tells us to rejoice in the Lord always. Christ has brought for us the materials gladness has made. New and happier thoughts, power, purpose, and hope. I don't have the hope of yesterday, but I have the hope of this moment. I have the hope that He lives within me. I have the hope that I'm going to help somebody today, and that makes me cheerful. I'm excited about serving my God. I'm pleased with where He's brought me from; I'm encouraged about what He is bringing me through, and I can hardly wait to get to where He's taking me.

Seek Self-control

The other element we need to look at is *forbearance*, which means "to refrain or control one's self." Forbearance shows us how to waive our just rights instead of always pushing them to the utmost.

It took me a long time to get there, but I'm half as dumb and twice as smart as 99% of the people think I am. In my younger days, I would get into an argument to prove my point. My wife would say, "Don't argue with him. He's going to argue till Jesus comes back." Have you been there? I have had to learn that just because we know something doesn't mean we have to push it off on somebody.

If we have a Word from God, then we should just sit on it for a few days and make sure it's from God and not from man. Before we give a prophetic word, we should sit on that thing like an egg and keep it warm until we are sure. That's why we should be in Christ. Forbearance. There are a lot of things I don't share.

Forbearance also means not returning evil for evil. I did a little job on the side not too long ago. I did it for exercise mostly, but there were a few bucks involved too. Now some folks perspire, but I sweat. I worked up a sweat that day. I worked hard. Afterwards, the people sent me a check with a little note attached. "My wife and I mowed our yard and half the neighbor's yard in one-third of the time. And we washed off the driveway. Don't come back." I picked up the phone and then thought, *No. What does that prove? Waste my two dollars to make a long distance call to prove what?* You don't return evil for evil.

We must be a people of few words. Let what we say mean something. It takes the character of God to hold back and not return evil for evil. It takes God's mercy to come in and say, *"Son, I know you want to whip that one, but just hold on. Let me work it out. I know your wife let you down this week. Hold on, I'll make it better."* It takes God's character to come in.

I'm finding that the more I get in Christ, the more I realize that He is at hand. He is there and sees everything that takes place. The Lord is not ignorant. He knows where I am. He knows what I'm dealing with and what I'm going through. He didn't just create me and leave me. In Hebrews 13:5 He said, "I will never leave thee nor forsake thee."

We must understand that the Lord is at hand. We don't have to return evil for evil. Very soon He is going to say, *"Come on, son. Do you hear that trumpet sound? I'm about to take you out of this mess."* That makes me cheerful. That makes me want to hold my peace and say, "God, let somebody see Christ in my life." Anyone can tell someone off. But not everyone can keep his mouth shut. It takes the character of God to come in and change a man.

Trust and Obey

Thirdly, for the gentleness of God to work out in my life, there must be a devout *trust*. Do you really trust the one to whom you gave your life? Do you really trust that His Word will keep you? You may be hurting, but the pain you are experiencing is not the issue. The issue is whether or not you are trustworthy and whether or not God is trustworthy. One person said, "I believe the Lord can heal my neighbor of cancer, but I just don't think He will heal me of a headache." That's not devout trustfulness. Trusting means that no matter what you walk through, no matter what you do or do not understand, you trust Him. There comes a time when you have to decide whom you trust. Philippians 4:7 says that the peace of God which passeth all understanding shall keep your hearts and minds through Christ Jesus.

In arguing this, the Apostle Paul does not teach us to have no care and to let everything drift. There are lots of folks letting everything drift. The end of the line is going to come for each of us someday. It may be at the age of forty, fifty, sixty, eighty, ninety, or one hundred. But the end will come. If we just drift through this life, then that's what we will have at the end of it. Nothing. He doesn't teach us not to care about anything. He teaches us to care—knowing that the Lord is at hand.

Do I trust Him enough to know He surrounds my life in every emergency? Even though I've never gone through this before, I'm going to remain cheerful because I'm devoted to Him. "Lord, I trust you, and I'm with you. I am full of your love and know you're going to send a redeemer. You're going to pick me up when I fall down."

We must do our best to give our cares to God. Sometimes all we can do with a situation is give it to God and trust that He will work it out. Then we can say, "I trust you, Lord, and by faith I see victory. By faith I'm going to be one of those peculiar types and smile about it." When we can let the cheerfulness of God begin to work in our lives, if any man be in Christ, he is a new creature.

I may know I should be down, but I can't stay down. I can't get down for standing up. Every time I get down, every time I hit the bottom, God comes in with His Word and says *"Son, look here, that word you couldn't understand a year ago? I am about to bring a revelation to you."*

To grow in grace I must have the characteristics of a gentle person. It doesn't mean I'm a wimp. It doesn't mean I'm sour. It doesn't mean I'm weak-kneed. I'm just gentle.

Peace in the Storm

The grand issue with gentleness is the peace of God. Let the peace of God calm your troubled waters. Let Him pick you up. The character of gentleness is godlike. The greatest way to live out the character of God is to be a cheerful believer, to be forever devoted.

You may admit, *Lord, I'm devoted, but I hate suffering.*

He says, *"My son, they persecuted me. Don't you think they're going to persecute you?"*

John 15 tells us to be willing to suffer to the extent that we partake of His sufferings. All of these sufferings in the end will make us gentle people, loving people, caring people. Even when we feel bad inside, somebody knows from the outside that God lives.

I see a lot of people who have just reason to be upset, hurt, and harmed. Yet I see the character of God in them. I see cheerfulness, gentleness, and happiness. That's the kind of person I want to go to. I don't want to go to an old grump who will tell me how bad everything is. I want someone to tell me where God brought him or her from. After all, that's why we go through the valley. He brings us out and builds our faith so we can help someone else.

The effect of gentleness is to stand sentinel and keep guard over the heart and mind. It is easy to be gentle when we are full of joy. When we are gentle, when people begin to pour their hearts out to us, instead of saying, "I've been through that," we can say, "I know God loves you." That's gentleness.

Have you had a tough time being a gentle believer? Ask God to help you be gentle. The old nature wants us to speak our minds and tell people off. Tell Him you desire gentleness, and ask Him to grow the characteristics of true Christianity in your life.

He desires to give us the spirit of gentleness, so we would be devoted to Him. He wants us to trust Him so He can trust us. It is unfair to ask God to trust us, if we don't trust Him.

Ask Him to help you hold your tongue and resist the temptation to tell everybody what you know. You don't always have to push your weight around or have the last word. Cheerfulness is one of the greatest ways to live out the Christian character. Live so that others see a person of integrity, a person who has direction, and someone who has settled things between himself and his Maker.

Chapter Ten

Rejoice in Hope

I hate the word *patience*, but I have to talk about it because the body of Christ lacks patience. Often people begin a new church, and if it doesn't grow overnight as they think it should, they say, "God's not in it. If it's of the Holy Ghost, the house would be full." Not necessarily so. The Bible says wherever two or three come together believing in His name, He is in their midst (Matt. 18:20). It has nothing to do with a full house.

As I prepared this study, it began to change my life. It helped me see things and helped me treat people differently. Several weeks later I started to wonder why my patience had been so tried. A minister friend of mine asked, "What are you preaching on?"

When I told him the topic was *patience*, he said, "No wonder. The enemy knows your ministry and knows you are about to move forward. He knows you're about to give a revelation of God's Word, so he's fighting to tear down your faith about the very thing you want to teach." The enemy doesn't want God's people to know we need to be patient.

Nobody likes patience. I feel I'm a very patient person—I just want it now. If I get it when I want it, I'm fine. God is humbling me, oh, is He humbling me.

We say, "Thank God for patience," but we don't even understand the kind of patience He has in mind. Romans 15:5 tells us God is patient: "Now the God of patience and consolation grant you to be likeminded one toward another according to Christ Jesus." The God of patience wants us to be like Him: patient towards our brothers and sisters in Christ and like-minded. He wants us to love one another as He loves us. In order to do that, we have to be patient with each other.

The greatest pitfall of my life is the foolishness of expectation. I've finally learned to be happy with folks and to expect out of them what I see. I have stopped expecting them to be something they are not. Now if I see anything more, I rejoice because God has blessed me and there is something new in them.

Running Ahead of God

After salvation, God expects us to grow and become rooted and grounded in the Word, but we want to go out and conquer the world before we're ready. We want to tell the world how to grow in grace before we understand grace.

Have you ever been upset because you felt the call in your life but the minister kept saying, "Let's be sure this is of God. Let's count the cost and make sure we don't get halfway through the battle and fall"? Have you ever fallen down in the battle and said, "God you left me"? No, He never told you to go. Patience.

Galatians 5:22–23 says, "But the fruit of the spirit is love, joy, peace, longsuffering, gentleness, goodness, faith, meekness, temperance: against such there is no law." It takes patience to be longsuffering. It takes patience to be gentle. It takes patience for faith. The moment I stand and say, "I have great faith," God's going to test me through patience. Do I really have faith in faith?

If God is patient, then He expects His people to be patient. Have you had to love an unloving person? It's tough, isn't it? It takes patience. Thank the Lord, my wife has been patient with me for almost eighteen years. I'm not as good as I need to be, but I'm a lot better than I was.

Patience in Tribulation

God works through us because He wants us able to face adversity with patience. I went to our church one Friday evening and thought, "I'm going to be a man of God and mow the lawn." As soon as I got out the old mower, I had to go buy a new seat because the old one had rotted off. When I got back, I cranked that thing up and headed across the field. Halfway across I realized one blade was turning and the other wasn't. Nothing like that had ever happened in the history of the mower—until I sat down on it. I went back to the barn and repaired the blade. I headed back out, and halfway across the field the fuel pump stopped pumping. Now I was out there rejoicing because I was going to share a word with the people of God about patience. I hopped off the mower and got my screwdriver. Have you ever had gasoline all over you in one-hundred-degree weather? It's really wonderful.

After I got it running again and made three or four strips across the field, I had a brainstorm. It must have been God. I decided I had better mow the front of the church first in case the old mower didn't make it. After ten strips across the front of the church, it stopped pulling. *Now what?* I thought. I looked down and saw three of the five belts just lying there. I put the belts back on, cranked up the mower, and when I came around, the belts flew off again. But I was patient. I put the belts back on and hooked up the fuel pump. It wouldn't pump. I stuck my hand on the exhaust. You could hear my skin sizzle like a piece of bacon.

Right about that time someone from the church pulled up and said, "Isn't this a beautiful day? Isn't God wonderful?"

I had to say, "Praise God, I am learning patience." But in my heart I was thinking, *Why don't we just shout for a while? I don't want to preach on patience. God, I'm tired of subjects that keep working on me. Give me something easier to deliver to the folks.*

To grow in grace, I have to conquer patience. I don't know if I have ever been madder than I was at that old mower. Then I got mad at myself—because I got mad. The whole time I rode that mower, I was going over in my mind what I would teach the people on Sunday. Finally I said, "God, this is turning my stomach. I'm going to have to change and take your Word to heart. I can't hear your Word and deny the truth. And I can't get up and preach one thing and go out and live something else."

God wants us to be patient in adversity. He wants His people to learn to walk through trials and temptations knowing that we may weep tonight, but joy is coming in the morning. Why do we automatically assume we're doing something wrong if we're going through the valley? We need to understand that God may be using us to show the enemy that we're settled and established. Did He not use Job? We've been made perfect through the blood.

Instead of trying to figure out what is wrong, get in your prayer closet. Turn that radio off and get in the Word. Say, "Lord, speak a word to me. Father, I've had so many prophetic words come my way that I don't know what is God and what is not because one contradicts another." If we would just hush and say, "Father, speak...."

We're in this thing together, and we're supposed to be family. The characteristics of a true Christian mean that when one hurts, we all hurt. I should be patient with you because you're walking through a trial, and that is my chance to build you up. Patience is a virtue, and patience is necessary.

Read Romans 12:12 and mark that verse. It says, "Rejoicing in hope; patient in tribulation; continuing instant in prayer." Think about what this means. What is it to rejoice? We can't rejoice if our senses are not pleased. We can't rejoice if we just live life according to our imaginations because then nothing ever becomes a reality. We can't rejoice in some farce; we have to rejoice in reality. If we get out of fantasy land, we have to say, "The Word says that if there is any good, then rejoice in that thing." So Lord, what is rejoicing? It is to rejoice on the positive side.

I can rejoice because my sorrow has been taken away. I can rejoice when my soul is content and satisfied. And the only way my soul can be satisfied is by God feeding me with His Word and filling an empty space with His love. When He takes the heart of a sinner and makes it a heart of God, I can rejoice. Yesterday I was dead and headed to a devil's hell, but today I'm saved, heading to God's kingdom. I can rejoice.

Rejoicing doesn't mean I don't feel pain. If I slam my finger in the door, I feel it. When you say something mean or ugly to me, I feel it. God didn't call me to be inhuman. He gave me a mind and emotions and feelings. I need patience so I will have hope—even when people are tearing me down. *Rejoicing in hope* means believing good things are coming.

I walked around a neighborhood in Wildwood some four and a half years ago, and it was my hope that there could be an Intensive Care Ministry. I rented a bingo hall and had hope that we could have something greater than the bingo hall. We moved to the storefront and had hope that God wouldn't leave us at that desolate place but would move us all to a place we could call home. It was a hope. Now we can look around at the hope God has made a reality.

We have been blessed, and blessings are given so we can give. I want to give and be a blessing. Recently I started looking for an electric piano for our church. The store said they would discount the one I wanted. It would only cost $4,000. I said, "Dear mercy, I can't go to the people and tell them we need $4,000. They won't understand. They'll probably tell me to get a five-gallon bucket and beat a tune on that."

For three months I talked with the folks at the music store and tried to find a way to buy this keyboard. We talked about trading in an old organ, but it was still too much money. One day the man called and said, "I have some good news about the piano. I sold it."

"What's good about that?" I asked.

"You don't understand. A gentleman walked in and bought the piano last week for $5,000. He came back today and said he loved it, but he wanted one with even more features which costs $9,000. I traded in the keyboard I just sold him and now I'm going to let the church have the blessing. That piano is used now, so I can't sell it as new. Bring me your old piano and $2,200, and I'll sell you the piano—and give you the $400 stand to go with it." Money is no object with God.

Keep Hope Alive

The enemy would love to steal our hope. Hope is an instinct of the soul. It's one of the strongest and most operative forces in our nature. If we got up in the morning and had lost all hope, we would be miserable and wretched, depressed and lifeless. We'd be nothing more than pieces of flesh with heartbeats. When a church or ministry loses hope, they may as well put up a sign that says, "We're dead. Don't come here. We've lost our hope." Few things are more distressing than the loss of hope. Loss of hope produces a spirit of depression and failure.

I've come close to losing my hope, and it's an eerie feeling. I went home one night, and my wife asked what was wrong. "I feel like I've been sliced open, and my guts have been ripped out."

Have you ever felt that way? That's the devil trying to steal your hope. It's not the preacher or the people you work with. It's not your companion or your children. It's not what you drive or what you wear or where you live. It has nothing to do with those things. The enemy hates your soul, and he's going to come against you and mess with your will and your emotions and try to cause you to lose hope. Unless you choose to fight him. "Lord, I have a headache and my back hurts, and I'm down and don't know how I'm going to make it next week, but I'm going to rejoice and hope that something good is coming my way. I'm miserable and wretched, and I don't know where to turn. I don't even know if I have a friend, but I'm rejoicing because a friend's about to come through the door." He said to rejoice in hope and be patient in tribulation.

One Sunday morning after services, I went straight home, lay down on the couch, and cried because the pain was unbearable. But that week I started reading about rejoicing and hope.

I walked into a place of business shortly after that and saw two riding lawn mowers sitting there. They were $1,100 each, but the sticker said 30% off. I went in and talked to the manager, a man I had worked for twenty years ago. "Your mower says 30% off," I said. "What's the best you can do for me?"

"Well, I'll give you my 10% discount, so it'll be 40% off."

I asked him to come outside and make sure we were talking about the same thing because that was an unbelievable price. I really didn't need a riding lawn mower, but how could I say no?

He had the lady ring it up, and when he went out to load the mower on my trailer he looked at the sticker again. "That sign says $30.00 off."

I said, "No, it says 30% off." I looked at it again. "Jiminy Cricket, that thing does say $30.00." I promise you before the good Lord in heaven, those little zeros looked like a percentage sign. I believe God messed with my head because He wanted to bless me. He wanted to give me something to rejoice about. Folks, if you wake up cross-eyed, then just know God's about to do something for you.

I said to the manager, "Can you live with that?"

He said, "We have already made the deal, and we can't go back on our word."

I loaded up the mower, and the first job I did was my neighbor's yard. God blessed me, so I was going to bless them. Then I realized I didn't need a riding mower for my small yard, but the church sure needed something to replace that miserable old thing we'd been using. God blessed me, and I was able to rejoice because He had restored my hope.

The devil will try to get us down on our faith and get us off balance. But in order to grow in grace, we have to be very patient with God because God is very patient with us.

You're going to fall down. You're going to get hurt. You're going to be miserable. You are going to have the nastiest fight at home you ever had. But if you can get over the natural way of living, God will build up your hope and your faith—even in the midst of the valley. He's going to give you a word to say. Don't lose your hope.

The devil's a liar and he hates you. The Bible says your adversary comes to steal, kill, and destroy. He wants to mess you up. But with God's Word, we're going to mess up what the enemy has been trying to do. We are going to rejoice in hope because that makes us patient in tribulation.

Patience—Right Now

What does the last part of Romans 12:12 say again? "Continuing in murmuring, complaining, griping and grumbling," right? Wrong. The Word says, "Instant in prayer."

I like being able to heat up a jar of water, throw some powder in it, and you've got coffee. Right now. I have to admit that even though I'm supposed to be patient and rejoice, I sometimes have a hard time with that. God says, "*OK, start rejoicing so I can help you be patient during your tribulation.*" That means things may not be coming together like I thought they would, but they are coming together. It means saying, "God, I don't know how you're going to do it, but I am confident you will."

When we begin to rejoice, He makes us patient in tribulation. We're always going to go through trials because God wants to show a lost and dying world that even through hard times His children have a promise. They have peace and joy and a reason to rejoice.

People will wonder how you can lose your car and still smile. Because God's going to send a better way. They will ask how you can have patience when you lose your job. Because God's got a better one. I'll tell you the truth, I wish someone would have preached this message to me ten years ago.

When God is passing by, we don't have time to go home and wonder, "Should I get beside myself so He can anoint and bless me, or should I shut up and keep my composure so nobody sees me with a tear in my eye." Beloved, when Jesus is passing by, we'd better be ready. When we're troubled in our minds and hearts, we should get ready because we have trouble for a reason.

Hebrews 12:1 challenges us to run with patience the race that is set before us. If we've lost our hope, we can't run. How did America gain its freedom? Because two or three fought for thirty minutes and then went home? No. Thousands gave their lives so you and I would have freedom. We must fight. We must keep the faith. We must rejoice in hope. I don't care if it seems like a fairy tale, believe it. Believe God is going to make a way. Rejoice in hope.

Some folks from our church had to put their truck in the shop and found out they needed two to three thousand dollars to rebuild the engine. He'd been out of work for a coon's age, and she'd been working day and night.

I said to them, "You just rejoice in hope."

"Pastor, do you know where the money's coming from?"

I said, "No, but God knows. He may send a stinking drunk or a suitcase on a roach's back. But He knows."

We need to get out of the gutter and be a people who rejoice in hope. He owns everything. It's His faith. It's His love and grace and mercy. Rejoice in hope.

Has the devil taken your hope away? Are you hurting? The day I went to the lawn mower shop, this church didn't know it needed a lawn mower, but God knew it needed one. He made a way. He's already opened the way for your miracle. I don't care what that doctor said. God said to rejoice in hope, and He would make you patient in tribulation. Be instant in prayer. Pour your heart out to God and see what He will do for you. Your patience may have been fought until you don't have any patience left, but let your faith be moved. Find something about which to rejoice. When you rejoice, He'll make you patient in tribulation and help you grow in grace.

Chapter Eleven

Instant Prayer

Have you ever watched a bird put into a cage for the first time? It goes crazy. It flies frantically—up and down, back and forth—trying to escape. But if you come back two or three days later, you find him sitting on a perch, whistling the same old tune.

Believers are a lot like that. When God allows tribulation to begin to work out our faith, what do we do? We flap our wings and say, "I don't like this pain. The whole world's caving in on me, and no one likes me." We fuss and rave and wear ourselves down spiritually. But if we are trying to be in Christ, three or four days later we find ourselves saying, "I don't like this cage God has me in, but I'm still singing 'What a Friend I Have in Jesus.'" When we live by the ways of the world, there is no cage. There is no real direction in our lives; we just live and go wherever and say and do whatever we want. When God begins to narrow our path in life, we have to learn how to respond.

I don't like the things the Lord has brought me through in the past ten years. There has been a lot of pain. But on the other side, I thank God He cared enough about me to put me in that cage. To be honest, I am getting used to that old cage.

Some of us need to get used to the cage. We have had it our way and called the shots for too long. Some of us have depended on our talents, gifts, and money for too long.

It's time to let God cage you. Quit trying to figure out what others are saying to you and say, "Lord, what are you saying to me? What do you want me to understand?" It is part of patience in tribulation.

It used to irritate me to see preachers more seasoned than myself walking around with a smile—even though I knew they were walking through tribulation. I thought, *Get off. There's a fake, if I ever saw one.* But as days go by, I'm seeing and feeling and experiencing God put a smile on my inner man in the midst of my own tribulation. It really doesn't matter what I have to walk through.

Change Hurts

It's painful when God begins to change our directions. Some areas of my life are difficult to change. I couldn't imagine if I were already sixty or seventy years of age. Common wisdom says you can't change some people. This is the way they are, and this is the way they are going to be. You might as well give up on them. I don't believe that. I've stood by the bedside of eighty-year-olds and prayed them through to Jesus. I believe anybody can change. I believe the Word is as much alive for a two-year-old as it is for a one-hundred-year-old. Change and growth are necessary for all of us. None of us are too old for Him to say, *"This is the way I want you to be."*

If we are patient in tribulation, then there is something else we need to know about Romans 12:12. Paul says, "Continuing instant in prayer." That's praying with faith and with a hardy desire. I have a desire to pray, but I don't always know the right words to pray.

I was ready to go to bed one night when something deep down asked, "Don't you want to pray?" My flesh said, "No," but the inner man said, "get up and walk around for a while and give Him praise." I had to do that before I could have peace.

Some of us ought to give up a bit of sleep for some prayer time. The Word says, "Continuing instant." Like instant cocoa or coffee, the hot water won't mean a thing until we put in the needed ingredient. Then we have something. We can't simply pray, "Now I lay me down to sleep, I pray the Lord my soul to keep," and figure we've prayed for the week. If we don't pray, we are hypocrites about our faith.

Too many believers think accepting Christ is all there is to it. The Word says, "Rejoicing in hope, and continuing instant in prayer." Do you know why we can't rejoice in hope? Because we're not praying people. We don't pray. We say we pray, but we really don't pray. If we did, we would be happy people because God would give us peace in our prayer time. He would give us the security of knowing that whatever else is going on in our lives, He will work it out. Continuing instant means always in your heart and spirit.

Prime the Pump

When a pump is used frequently, little pain is necessary to get water. You just walk out, pump it a time or two, and—*boop*—there's water. But when that pump doesn't get used for a few days or weeks, you can wear yourself out trying to get a cup of water. It's the same principle with prayer. We are exhorted to pray. When we don't, it seems to take a long time to get through. But when we pray daily and continue instant in our prayers, the words just begin to pour out.

Then there are the prayers we never put into words. We must be careful not to twist Scripture here. Continuing instant in prayer means to carry on. It does not mean the cashier stops to pray in the middle of ringing up your groceries. The firefighter doesn't stop and bow his head while a house burns up. Some prayers are never spoken. When we are right with Jesus Christ, there is an ongoing prayer deep down inside us.

On the Mariner's compass, the needle always wants to point north. While it's busy telling the captain which way the ship should go, it wants to point north. It never speaks a word; it simply does its job.

There are some who say, "I can't work and hold down a job because I'm a prayer warrior." Baloney. God never said to forsake our obligations in life. He said if a man doesn't work, he doesn't eat (2 Thessalonians 3:10). Some wonder, "How can I be a man of God if I'm always busy working?" God will make a way. He will make a prayer that continues.

People have said they never see me praying. It's not anyone's business to see me praying. You will know soon enough if I pray or not. And I'll know if you pray. I'll know by your conversation, and you'll know by mine. You will know by my leadership, and I'll know by the way your family acts. It makes a difference when our hearts are right with Christ. Whether it is a verbal prayer or an instant prayer in the inner man, there is always a prayer going forth. Always. Always. Always.

I have an old wind-up clock in my garage. I walked by it a few days ago and wound it up. Wouldn't you know, it started keeping time. I walked by it last night and there wasn't a tick or a tock in the whole neighborhood. Why? I forgot to wind it up. That's the way it is with our spiritual lives. If we don't keep our spiritual clocks wound, we'll stop growing. If we don't communicate with our Father, He won't communicate with us.

Some prayers are hindered but not defeated. Here's where a lot of us live. When our prayers aren't answered, we assume God either doesn't hear us or He doesn't care about us. Maybe the problem is a selfish prayer. "Lord, you said you would bless me, so I want that new Cadillac." That is not what the Word is talking about.

I can be prosperous in my prayer life. I don't have a real fancy home, but I am prosperous. I have peace and joy. When tribulation comes, He is teaching me patience. He is showing me some things that are greater than silver or gold. What matters is what's going on inside my heart.

I watched a bird take off as though he were flying to the heavens. He flew for a while and then he seemed to rise up and fall back, rise up and fall back. Pretty soon a strong eastern wind beat him back to the ground. He rested for a while and tried to catch his breath. Then he revived himself and—as though he had heard a word from an angel of the Lord—he took off straight to the heavens. That's the way it is with our prayers. Sometimes we pray, but the enemy intercepts. He interferes and hinders our prayers. When we get knocked down, the Father sends His angels to whisper, "Pray it one more time."

I heard a preacher say you shouldn't ask God for the same thing twice. If I had not asked my daddy some things four, five, or six times, I would never have had them. If he's my example as an earthly father, then my heavenly Father must love it when I have enough faith to keep coming back, time and time again. My prayer may have been hindered, but I have enough faith to know it hasn't been defeated.

Romans 8:38 says, "For I am persuaded that neither death, nor life, nor angels, nor principalities, nor powers, nor things present, nor things to come, nor height, nor depth nor any other creature, shall be able to separate us from the love of God, which is in Christ Jesus our Lord." I am satisfied and persuaded of that. The devil may hinder me, but God is in control. Isaiah 54:17 says, "No weapon that is formed against thee shall prosper; and every tongue that shall rise against thee in judgment thou shalt condemn." Thank God for prayer.

"Now I Lay Me Down to Sleep...."

There are also nightly prayers. It is said that John Quincy Adams never went to sleep until he had prayed a prayer learned in childhood. When was the last time you breathed a prayer before you went to sleep? Some may answer, "But every time I lay my head down to pray, I fall asleep in my prayer." I'd rather go to sleep praying than worrying. I've gotten up in the morning and said, "Lord, where were we?" If you go to bed worrying, you will wake up worrying. But if you go to bed praying, you will wake up saying, "Lord, I don't know if I completed my prayer, but I thank you for communing with me. Thank you for a good night's rest." We should pray rather than fuss ourselves to sleep.

I read about a man named Fletcher whose whole life was a life of prayer. His mind was so intensely fixed upon God that he would not get out of his chair without asking God where He wanted him to go. His friends said his typical greeting was to ask if he had met them praying. He was so settled and set in his faith that in the middle of a conversation he would stop and say, "Where are our hearts now?"

When someone in the church catches you in the back room and begins to unload on you, look them right in the eyes and say, "Where are our hearts now?"

Never Quit

Pray without ceasing. When do my brothers and sisters fall? When I quit praying for them. When do I fall? When others quit praying for me. When we quit praying and start fussing, then we've missed it. We are to be people of prayer, continuing instant in prayer. Always.

Let's look at three words: constant, instant, expectant. The Greek word *instant* means "always applying strength in prayer." Blessed is the man whose strength is in thee. One gentleman uses the analogy of a hunting dog. The dog won't give up on the chase until he collects what he has been chasing. Have you ever seen a hunting dog stop in the middle of the race?

I was at a ball game not too long ago. One of the boys got a little winded and just walked out of the game. The coach said, "What are you doing? I've never seen a player check himself out of the game."

Being instant in prayer has a certain sense of agony. We must go to God with our whole hearts. We're going to agonize with God and never give up.

Look at the word *constant*. Go back to the hunting dog illustration. We see him rushing like the wind after his game. But if he gives up in the middle of a fight, that old hound is worthless. He must keep running if he is going to catch his prey.

In the iron industry it is a sign of failure if the furnaces are blown out. But when business flourishes, the fires blaze day and night. So it is when my soul is flourishing. There is a vision and a dream. Something happens when we continue instant in prayer and are constant about our faith.

Don't quit praying. Don't give up. We often bring our burdens and lay them on the altar saying, "Lord, I really trust you," but on the way out we sheepishly take them back home with us. Then we wonder why we don't feel like we were in the house of God. It is because we refuse to be changed. We refuse to pray and be constant about our faith. People say, "I don't feel sanctification working in my life." I don't doubt it a bit. They won't be still and let God work sanctification long enough. We must continue instant in our prayers.

Let's look at the word *expectant*. It's not in the text, but it must be there because we can't have instancy or constancy unless there is an expectation that God can and will give that which we seek. Go back to the hunting dog again. He would not run at so great a rate if he did not expect to seize his prey. If some people looked out for answers to prayer, they might soon have them, for they could answer their prayers themselves. If I want to get out of the poverty level, I need to work harder.

I'll be honest with you. I'm not against faith preachers, but there is more to it than just faith. If we want our households to fare better, we need to go back to when everything was working. Go back to the principles you were taught in the home. Pick them up and put them into practice. Some of us need to look in the mirror and say, "You know what, Self, you were stupid." This works for me because it makes me face reality. It makes me want to go back to my prayers and expect an answer from God.

A father was praying one night and said, "Lord, you know the poor and needy out there. Lord, I pray you would bless them and meet their needs."

After the father finished, his little son said, "Daddy, I wish I had your money."

"Well son, what would you do with my money?"

"I sure would answer your prayers."

Another gentleman was reading out the list of special needs one Wednesday evening. One said an elderly lady in the church needed her roof repaired. He began to read out the request and then he stopped and said, "Wait a minute, I need not bother the Lord with this one. I'll just go take care of it."

A poor man offered this prayer: "Oh Lord, give me grace to fill my need of your grace. Give me grace to ask for thy grace. Give me grace to receive thy grace and when in thy grace thou has given me grace, give me grace to use thy grace."

If you expect God to help you rejoice in hope and be patient in tribulation, you are going to have to do something. You can't just sit there and say, "God, move me if you can." He'll let you sit there and rot. You may say that's harsh, but it's the truth. Patch the neighbor's roof. It won't break you. Give a little boy a quarter. It won't hurt you. Put your arm around somebody and say, "You know, the Lord loves you." It won't harm you. Walk up to a stranger and say, "I don't know you, but I'm expecting God to do something powerful in your life."

Rejoicing in hope. Patient in tribulation. Constant in prayer.

Chapter Twelve

The Spirit of Forgiveness

In order for virtue and faith, gentleness, meekness, and patience to operate in my life, something else must be at work and that is a spirit of forgiveness. Too many churches today have plenty of critics but no spirit of forgiveness. We are so busy trying to change what's on the outside that we're missing what is wrong on the inside. It is much easier for me to criticize my children than to criticize myself. It's much easier to judge than to have a spirit of forgiveness. A forgiving spirit doesn't come easy.

When we hold a grudge, but call ourselves righteous, we are two-faced. Unfortunately, there are lots of two-faced believers walking around. We call ourselves one thing, but there is no evidence around the altar. We say we believe people get saved, and we believe in the baptism of the Holy Spirit. We believe somebody is going to receive a supernatural and divine miracle from God himself, but we never see it happen. Why? Because there is no spirit of forgiveness. We are quick to say, "God bless me and mine." Lots of people pray for their enemies, not because they want to see their enemies blessed, but because the Word says it'll heap hot coals on their heads (Rom. 12:20). So we pray, "Oh God, turn up the flame—I'm praying for my enemy." We pray with an ill attitude.

What is forgiveness? It is the act of excusing and pardoning others in spite of their shortcomings and errors. As a theological term, forgiveness refers to God's pardon of the sins of humankind. Folks read lots of books, but the only Book in this world that teaches true, unadulterated forgiveness is the Word of God. You might as well throw out all the rest. Get into the Word and ask God to teach you about forgiveness. We've looked too long and too hard for other answers. We have even gone to psychiatrists so they would make us feel better about the grudges we're holding against our neighbors. Get into the Word instead. Psalm 51:1 says, "Have mercy upon me, O God, according to thy lovingkindness: according unto the multitude of thy tender mercies blot out my transgressions."

I am sick and tired of people preaching that God is a judge. God is a righteous and holy God, but from the beginning He has had a spirit of forgiveness. We've made God a monster that He's not. He said if we refuse to change, we will face consequences. But first and foremost, He has a spirit of forgiveness. When we say, "God is my Savior, my king, and my hero, but I hate you," we give God a bad name. When we don't forgive, in essence we're saying, "I hate you."

Not long ago my wife suggested we make a list of everyone we need to forgive. I said, "Well, you may need a book, but I only have two I've got to forgive." I was feeling very proud of myself. Several days later I was out walking, and I prayed, "Lord, I forgive so-and-so, and Lord, I forgive this one and that one. Praise God, holy and righteous. Lord, I'm so obedient. I'm a forgiver!"

The Lord said, "*Wait a minute. What about brother so-and-so?*"

"Well, Lord, I forgive them—"

The Lord interrupted. "*What about sister so-and-so? And brother so-and-so?*"

I was there for quite some time. I've had to forgive more people than I realized. You see, I had said, "Holy Spirit, speak to me. If I have ought against my brother, remind me." He did. The names began to roll through my mind like a scroll. "Lord, can you slow down? I can't keep up."

We call ourselves holy and righteous, and we expect God to forgive us, but we won't forgive others. When we won't forgive others, we can't receive the blessings God has for us. We won't receive blessings from others, either. If I hold a grudge against my neighbor, he will never mow my lawn.

God is love according to 1 John 4:8. That tells me a spirit of forgiveness comes from a heart full of love. When Adam and Eve fell, God knew He needed to send a Savior. And He knew that that Savior would forgive man of his sins. All through the Old Testament we find sacrifices made with the blood of animals. Throughout the Old Testament there was also the promise of the coming Messiah. With the promise came a promise of forgiveness.

God said essentially, "*I know you need it, and because forgiveness is on my heart, I'm going to send my only begotten Son, born of a virgin. Not only will I send Him, but He will suffer for the sins of this world. They will beat Him, curse Him, slap Him, and hang Him on a cross to die a brutal death. His blood and water will pour into this earth. But then He will come out of the tomb and be lifted up to sit at the right hand of the Father because you need forgiveness.*" He promised it. And God is not a liar. Hebrews 6:18 says it was, and is, impossible for God to lie.

But You Promised

When you receive a promise and you don't see it fulfilled immediately, what do you do? If you go back to God with the wrong attitude and say, "But you said...," in essence, you're telling God He lied to you. The Word says He is not a God who lies. He's just trying to work something out in our lives. When I preach about miracles or divine healing, don't you know I'm going to get sick as a dog? Sometimes we have to walk through the valley of the shadow of death. Some of us need to know we have power and authority over the enemy. We are not subject to him; he is subject to us.

I've been kicked around long enough. I'm not going to go through the week fussing, griping, and complaining because I don't feel good. That just means somebody is going to be saved or healed. That means there will be miracles in the house. To whom much is given, much is required.

If God's going to do something supernatural in your life, get ready. He's going to put you before men. Sometimes I wish He'd put me before a tree instead. He knows man's going to rub you the wrong way, so He tests you to see if you have that forgiving spirit. And if you don't have that spirit, guess what? Someone else will come along to mess with you. They will keep coming until you prove you can forgive no matter what they do to you. He promised that He would forgive you. He wouldn't give His Son to die on the cross for our sins and then create a place like heaven for us only to quit. He wouldn't bring us this far and then say, "Ha, ha." Why wouldn't He quit? It's simple: He promised. When God wanted to destroy the children of Israel, Moses said, "The nations will say you are a false God if you do that. There is too much at stake."

God is not out to destroy you. There is too much at stake. Some of you live as though you are defeated. You're not defeated; you're just walking through the valley. God wants to get you to the place where you can put a smile on your face no matter what you are going through. God wants you to quit living in pain. When you live in pain and don't have that spirit of forgiveness, it begins to eat you up like a cancer. Your immune system gives up and your bones begin to deteriorate. Your heart begins to act crazy. Your veins begin to stop up. If you'd fill your veins with the Holy Ghost and fire, nothing would stop up those veins.

I once went into business with a partner. I borrowed a few thousand dollars to get things ready, and just before we were to open the doors, he quit. He just walked out. Aren't you glad God doesn't work that way? God won't bring you this far and say, "OK, I'm finished with you." You are the only one who can destroy the spirit of God within you. I can be happy or I can be sad. No sooner do I forgive someone than something reminds me of that individual. Then the devil comes up and says, "See, you can't forgive them." I forgive in Jesus' name. Isaiah 41 says if I forgive long enough, they'll be gone. I'm going to come against that thing and it's going to be gone. Have you ever waited for that to happen? Come on, be truthful.

God is a God of forgiveness and He proved it. Jacob was a wicked man. He wrestled against the angel of God. He deceived his brother and lied to his father. But the Word tells us that God forgave him. God even forgives liars. Look at Isaiah. He began to talk as the people talked and do as the people did. But here's where a lot of us miss it. In the sixth chapter, Isaiah admitted he was wrong.

If I hold a grudge, I have to admit I was wrong. My own brothers and sisters have hurt me. I want my family to be together, but we can't be until I truly forgive. Then God can deal with them. Isaiah said, "Woe is me! for I am undone; because I am a man of unclean lips, and I dwell in the midst of a people of unclean lips..." (Isa. 6:5a). Some of you need to quit hanging around with certain people. If all you get is stinking, rotten conversation, then find yourself new friends.

Isaiah 6:5b continues, "For mine eyes have seen the King, the Lord of hosts." There is coming a time when you will see the King of Kings and the Lord of Lords. And for once you're going to quit accusing everyone else and say, "I've seen the Lord." How do you know when you're seeing the Lord? When that tear begins to rise up, you know you're about to see Jesus. "Then flew one of the seraphims unto me, having a live coal in his hand, which he had taken with the tongs from off the altar: and he laid it upon my mouth, and said, Lo, this hath touched thy lips; and thine iniquity is taken away, and thy sins are purged" (vv. 6–7).

Forgiveness Demands Action

God doesn't forgive you without giving you a command. He won't forgive you without commissioning you. If you say you are saved but don't know your calling, you haven't been listening. Isaiah 6:8 says, "And I heard the voice of the Lord, saying, 'Whom shall I send, and who will go for us?'" The one who was just forgiven. The one who just said, "Woe is me." If you admit you were wrong, God is going to send you. Isaiah said, "Here am I Lord, send me." Not only did God forgive him but also He used him.

God told Jonah to deliver the word of the Lord to Ninevah. Jonah went out and paid for a boat ride to get away from the presence of God. He tried to hide from his anointing, his calling.

You can run, but you can't hide. I tried to find a pile of rocks to hide under, but the Word says, "They that worship him, must worship him in spirit and in truth." Jeremiah 20:9 said it this way: "It's like fire shut up in my bones." You may be hurt and feel you don't have a word to tell, but there is a word hidden. You can't hide from the word that's been planted. If He called you, you are going to have to be willing to say, "Lord, I'm sorry for holding that grudge against others."

Jonah ended up in the belly of a whale. Have you ever felt you are in the belly of a whale? What caused that whale to get sick and throw Jonah up? Jonah repented. When you repent, the devil can't keep his hands on you. He's got to throw you up and let you go. Sounds gross, doesn't it? It's no more gross than being in the valley of the shadow of death and not knowing your way out. It's no more gross than hiding in self-righteousness, only to find you're covered with sin.

After Jonah repented, he went to Ninevah and said in essence, "People, listen to me. Boy, do I have a word for you." Had he gone to Ninevah in the beginning he might have said, "Well, God sent me with the word." But after he went through the valley of the shadow of death, he spoke with such authority that the people listened. They even commanded the animals to fast. The people of Ninevah received the word, and because one man prayed for forgiveness, 600,000 were saved. Let me put it in your lap. There are 600,000 out there waiting on you to ask for forgiveness.

God can't use you until you are forgiven. What sins and grudges stand in the way of God's blessing on your life?

Chapter Thirteen

Sin's Payment

Sometimes I say, "Lord, remember that sin I committed and asked you to forgive?"

He'll say, "*Huh? What sin? You're my creation, and yes, you failed, but I forgave you.*"

I thank God He doesn't remember my past. If He doesn't remember it, I must not clog up my being with yesterday either.

Why do we clog up with what's wrong? We need to get excited about what is right. In marriage counseling, one of the first things I do is ask both husband and wife to write down all the good things about their spouses. Then I ask them to write down the bad things. Almost every time, the good things far outnumber the bad. So I ask, "Now, what is the problem?"

Often, the problem is that we would rather argue over what's wrong. We say we want to be set free, but we really don't. We proclaim a false gospel if we say we are free yet we're miserable. We can't even sleep at night because of what goes on in our minds. If you can't sleep well at night, there is a reason for it.

One of the things I want you to understand about the spirit of forgiveness is that the initiative came from God. It didn't come from man. Someone didn't sit down and write a book that explains forgiveness and how to forgive. It was God's idea. As stated before, 1 John 4:8 says, "God is love." If God is a God of love, and if forgiveness has to do with a spirit of love, then God must be the recipe. Because of His love I'm forgiven and set free by the blood of Jesus Christ. John 3:16 said, "For God so loved the world that he gave his only begotten son that whosoever believeth in him should not perish but have everlasting life." Colossians 2:13 says, "And you, being dead in your sins and the uncircumcision of your flesh, hath he quickened together with him, having forgiven you all trespasses." It was God who forgave.

Look at the prodigal son. The father was raking the yard and looking down the street one day when he saw what appeared to be his son. That boy had spent all he had and half of what his father had. He had slept in the hog pen and eaten with the hogs. You know when you sleep in a hog pen, you smell worse than a hog—and a hog smells bad enough. But he came home, and his father said to the servants, "Go kill the fatted calf. Get the best one in the field. My son's come home." God gets excited when his children come home. It was His idea to forgive.

We need that same spirit of forgiveness. Nehemiah 9:17 says, "But thou art a God ready to pardon, gracious and merciful, slow to anger, and of great kindness, and forsookest them not." He is a God of grace and pardon. Sin deserves divine punishment because it is a violation of God's holy character, but His pardon is gracious. Because of sin we deserve to die. But God gave His Son's life that we could live. Romans 5:6–8 says:

> For when we were yet without strength, in due time Christ died for the ungodly. For scarcely for a righteous man will one die: yet peradventure for a good man some would even dare to die. But God commendeth His love toward us, in that, while we were yet sinners, Christ died for us.

Thank God He gave His Son. Thank God He knew we were going to fail. Thank God He knew there were troubled days coming. God knew we were going to need a Savior, and He did not want to give us a rock out of the field. He wanted to give us His very best, His only begotten Son so we would understand His forgiveness. Sin demands that something die. God said, *"I'm going to have my Son die, so you might have life. Oh, not just life, but life more abundant."*

The Willing Substitute

In order for God to forgive sin, two conditions are necessary. First, a life must be taken as a substitute for that of a sinner. Leviticus 17:11 says, "For the life of the flesh is in the blood: and I have given it to you upon the altar to make an atonement for your souls: for it is the blood that maketh an atonement for the soul." Hebrews 9:22 says, "And almost all things are by the law purged with blood; and without the shedding of blood is no remission." Instead of taking our lives, God gave His Son's life that we would have life.

We can't come to Christ unless we come with a spirit of repentance. But we can't have a spirit of repentance until we realize something's wrong. When we admit that only God can clean up the mess, we have the spirit of repentance.

We also need the spirit of faith. When we come in a spirit of repentance and faith, He is just and faithful to forgive. Mark 1:4 says, "John did baptize in the wilderness, and preach the baptism of repentance for the remission of sins." James 5:15 tells us, "And the prayer of faith shall save the sick, and the Lord shall raise him up; and if he have committed sins, they shall be forgiven him."

If somebody has sinned against me, I want to be able to forgive that person. I want to be like Jesus. I believe that when Jesus had a chance to sleep, He slept well. Why? Because He didn't hold grudges. He was an example of forgiveness. Some of you are going to have to back up a few years and start forgiving.

Connected Threads

In the New Testament, forgiveness is directly linked to Christ. Acts 5:31 says, "Him hath God exalted with his right hand to be a Prince and a Savior, for to give repentance to Israel, and forgiveness of sins." Colossians 1:14 says, "In whom we have redemption through his blood, even the forgiveness of sins." We can't have God unless we have Christ. We can't have the Holy Spirit unless we have God the father, God the Son, and God the Holy Ghost. I feel sorry for people who preach and believe only part of the trinity. There are times I call on the great Holy Ghost to help me out. There are other times I sit and weep, saying, "Jesus, Savior, the compassionate one, the great physician, come and touch me." Then there are times I say, "God, I need your help." It was God who made the mountain move. It was Christ who spoke the word, but it was God the father in His infinite wisdom and power who said, "Be moved."

Forgiveness is wrapped up in Christ. Look at His sacrificial death on the cross. Romans 4:24 tells us, "But for us also, to whom it shall be imputed, if we believe on him that raised up Jesus our Lord from the dead." Also, 2 Corinthians 5:15 says, "And that he died for all, that they which live should not henceforth live unto themselves, but unto him which died for them, and rose again." That is a powerful verse. It means to give it up and quit trying to live for ourselves. To live this verse, we can't have it our way and God's way, too. He died for us. If we have accepted forgiveness for our sins, it's time to put on the coat of righteousness and say, "Lord, I'm going to live it your way, even though that may be different from my way. It may be difficult at times, but I'm going to live your way."

Christ made the ultimate sacrifice. Some of us go around complaining about the sacrifices we have made. None of us have made a sacrifice like Christ did. Have they beaten and cursed you? Have they spit upon you and pierced your side until the fluid ran out of your body? Have you gone to hell? Have you conquered death and ascended to the right hand of the father? I don't think so.

The Perfect Lamb

Christ was the morally perfect sacrifice. Romans 8:3 says, "For what the law could not do, in that it was weak through the flesh, God sending his own Son in the likeness of sinful flesh, and for sin, condemned sin in the flesh." There is no better sacrifice than Christ. We don't have to call 1-900-Psycho. All we need to do is call on Jesus. He was perfect. He knew the law was weak and that it couldn't do everything. So God planned to give His Son as the perfect sacrifice. He was the final and ultimate fulfillment of the Old Testament sacrifices. Thank God for that perfect sacrifice!

Hebrews 10:18 says, "Now where remission of these is, there is no more offering for sin." Aren't you glad we're not under the law anymore? Aren't you glad that when you do wrong, the preacher can't take you out and stone you? Think about that. I figure by now, I would have been stoned at least a couple hundred times. The world may hate me and turn against me, but I thank God Jesus gave His life so I could be forgiven of my sins. I have hope and peace today because of His sacrifice.

By His death, Christ took us out of the actions of the law and put us into the actions of grace. Thank God for grace. Christ bore the law's death penalty against sinners. (see Romans 5:10–11) Those who trust in his sacrifice are freed from the penalty. Since He gave His life and shed His blood, we can have that same spirit of forgiveness and say, "Father forgive me." That's what the shedding of the blood does for us: it frees us from the penalty of sin.

By faith sinners are forgiven. Paul calls it justified in Romans 3:28 when he says, "Therefore we conclude that a man is justified by faith without the deeds of the law." We are not bound; we are forgiven. We are bound only if we haven't accepted forgiveness. It's a slap in God's face when people say, "I believe God can forgive everyone else, but He can't forgive me." God is a big God. He is such an awesome God that He not only gave His only Son to die but also He raised Christ from the dead that we might live. He is an example of the life we are to live.

God is a God of grace. He is a God of mercy. He is a God of forgiveness. He will pardon that which is wrong in your life. What a precious gift we have been given! Before the day is out you may do something you shouldn't. But, with a heart and spirit of repentance, all you have to say is, "Father, I'm so sorry. I didn't mean to say that. I didn't mean to hurt that person or think those thoughts." Aren't you glad that we are forgiven?

Demands of Grace

I don't like it when people get in my face and make demands. I don't like it at all. The God of grace makes a demand on us we cannot ignore. It's not optional. He demands that we forgive others.

Take an honest look back over the years. Did someone hurt you? You've said with your mouth, "I forgive," but every time you see that person or hear that person's name, deep down in your heart something grabs and grips you. The spirit says you haven't really, truly forgiven because when you have, peace and joy come. Happiness comes.

I'm going to share a scripture passage with you that has rocked my life. It has made me put a demand on myself to forgive and forget. Matthew 18:23–35 says:

> Therefore is the kingdom of heaven likened unto a certain king, which would take account of his servants. And when he had begun to reckon, one was brought unto him, which owed him 10,000 talents. But forasmuch as he had not to pay, his lord commanded him to be sold, and his wife, and children, and all that he had, and payment to be made. The servant therefore fell down, and worshipped him, saying, "Lord, have patience with me, and I will pay thee all." Then the lord of that servant was moved with compassion, and loosed him, and forgave him the debt. But the same servant went out, and found one of his fellowservants, which owed him an 100 pence: and he laid hands on him, and took him by the throat, saying, "Pay me that thou owest." And his fellowservant fell down at his feet, and besought him, saying, "Have patience with me, and I will pay thee all." And he would not: but went and cast him into prison, till he should pay the debt. So when his fellowservants saw what was done, they were very sorry, and came and told unto their lord all that was done. Then his lord, after that he had called him, said unto him, "O thou wicked servant, I forgave thee all that debt, because thou desirest me: Shouldest not thou also have had compassion on thy fellowservant, even as I had pity on thee?" And his lord was wroth, and delivered him to the tormentors, till he should pay all that was due unto him. So likewise shall my heavenly Father do also unto you, if ye from your hearts forgive not every one his brother their trespasses.

Don't miss what is being said here. The king forgave that which was owed him because the servant humbled himself. "Please have mercy upon me," he cried. God the king was moved with compassion when He saw we needed a Savior. So much so that He gave His only begotten Son. That's a move and a half if you ask me. His answer was: *"Because of your crying out to me and your humbleness, I forgive you."* Then the servant went out and found someone who owed him money and grabbed him by the nap of the neck. He would not forgive, and the king got angry. He said, "Because you won't forgive, the tormentors are coming."

When I began to study that passage, the Spirit of the Lord said, *"Son, do you know what 'the tormentors' means? Because you won't forgive, sickness is going to come. You won't be able to sleep at night because you are so bound up with grief and sorrow over what you're holding against someone. You won't be able to hold a decent conversation because you're eaten up with what the past has brought you. If you don't forgive like I forgive, the tormentors are coming to your home. Your mind's going to be baffled and you won't know if you're coming or going."*

You may be wondering why you can't get on your feet. Maybe it's because you won't forgive those who have cursed you or wrongfully used you. Christ said if we're not willing to forgive, the tormentors will come to our homes. We are going to suffer in our bodies, and our finances are never going to be what they should be. When you run from church to church, preacher to preacher, husband to husband, or wife to wife—but you can't forgive yesterday—you're just taking the tormentors right along with you. When you get to the other church and get good and settled, guess what? The tormentors show up on both sides of you and say, "Look here, you think that other preacher was bad...."

We must forgive so our homes will be the way they should be. My wife will tell you that I have hurt her. Thankfully, she will also tell you she has forgiven me. That is why we have peace and unity. The tormentor doesn't live at our house. He's not welcome there. If you want the tormentor to go, you've got to be willing to forgive.

How Many Times?

Luke 6:37 says, "Judge not, and ye shall not be judged: condemn not, and ye shall not be condemned: forgive, and ye shall be forgiven." Very simply, you reap what you sow. Jesus placed no limits on the extent to which Christians are to forgive others.

Peter asked Jesus, "Lord, how oft shall my brother sin against me, and I forgive him? Till seven times?" Jesus answered, "Until seventy times seven" (Matt. 18: 21–22). He said we should forgive over and over and over. As soon as you forgive someone, the tormentor is going to come and say, "You didn't really forgive." I may have to forgive him again and again until I don't even remember what he did to me. That's the revelation of God's Word. My wife has had to forgive me a whole bunch of times, on the same issue, to get peace in our home.

A forgiving spirit shows that one is a true follower of Christ. Matthew 5:43–46 says:

> Ye have heard that it hath been said, Thou shalt love thy neighbor, and hate thine enemy. But I say unto you, Love your enemies, bless them that curse you, do good to them that hate you, and pray for them which despitefully use you, and persecute you; That ye may be the children of your Father which is in heaven: for he maketh his sun to rise on the evil and on the good, and sendeth rain on the just and on the unjust. For if ye love them which love you, what reward have ye? Do not even the publicans the same?

The Lord is saying, *"So what if you love someone who loves you?"*

At times, I have seen greater love in the camp of sinners than in the camp of God's people. That's sad. God is saying, *"If you know I love you and you love me back, big deal. But, you've really proven something when you love the person who despitefully used you, wronged you, hurt you, and harmed you."* That's what Scripture teaches.

The initiative of forgiveness comes from God, a God of grace and pardon. It doesn't come from Buddha or some Pharisee. It comes directly from God, and it was provided through Christ's death on the cross. After we accept God's forgiveness, He demands that we forgive others. He didn't say forgive if we want to or if we feel like it. He said do it. I am amazed that He gave us the choice to be saved, but He demands that we forgive. And if we don't forgive, the tormentors are coming.

To be a person of forgiveness, you have to take action. In James 2:20, the Bible says faith without works is dead. Now that I know God demands forgiveness, I have to do something when He reminds me of those I need to forgive. I have to say, "Lord, I've stepped out of bondage. I've closed the door and padlocked it behind me so the tormentors can no longer come. I'm going to put wheels on my faith."

Ask the Lord to forgive your unforgiving spirit. Thank Him for His Word. And when He brings to mind someone you are holding a grudge against, forgive that person. Speak it to the Lord. He knows your heart.

Chapter Fourteen

The Radiant Life

This is not heaven, but I believe we can have a taste of it on earth by the way we live, the attitudes we have, and the things we know about God and His Word. We don't have to live in a little box, but we can enjoy the good things in this life if we get out of the natural and into the supernatural. That scares a lot of folks, though, because they think that means becoming a fanatic. Frankly, there are worse things we could be.

We have studied the difference between knowing *of* Christ and knowing Christ. To have the characteristics of a true Christian, you start with birth, and birth comes through obedience to the Word of God. You can't have God or know God without His Word. Someone can share his experiences in Christ with you, and you can repent and by faith ask Christ to come into your heart and save you. But from that moment on you have to get to know God on your own. You cannot live off someone else's faith. You can't live off their glory or anointing either. You have to get your own anointing. You can't look at my marriage and say you want yours to be like mine. You can't have my marriage; you have to find your own. This marriage is between me and my Lord and Savior. You have to gain your own, and the only way that happens is if you get into the Word.

After the new birth comes spiritual growth. As we studied, 2 Peter 3:18 tells us to "grow in grace, and in the knowledge of our Lord and savior Jesus Christ. To Him be glory both now and for ever. Amen." God is calling His Church to be different from anything the world has ever experienced. But before you can be different, you have to do what the first part of the scripture said. You have to grow in grace.

If you're going to grow in grace, you must first know what that involves. When somebody puts a new recipe on my table and says, "try it," I'm skeptical. Before I dip my spoon in, I want to know what's in it. There are too many surface Christians. If you're going to dedicate your life to serving Christ, you need to know whom you serve. You need to dig deeper into His Word.

Growing in grace includes many things. We found there must be virtue, which is moral excellence or goodness. We found faith, a belief in or confident attitude towards God involving commitment to His will for one's life. We found meekness, an attitude of humility towards God and gentleness toward people which springs from a recognition that God is in control. We found there must be gentleness, which is kindness, consideration, a spirit of fairness, and compassion. We found there must be patience in grace. There is forbearance under suffering and endurance in the face of adversity. And we found we can't grow in grace until there is a spirit of forgiveness because as believers, we must be willing to forgive each other.

Forgiveness begins at home. We can't forgive each other until we can forgive the members of our own household. We must ask for it and give it. Men, if you apologize, it does not mean you are weak-kneed. The Bible says the man who gets on his knees before Christ is a man who can stand up to anything. We need to humble ourselves so we can be the men of God He has called us to be. Sometimes we all need an attitude adjustment.

Useful Servants

In addition to the spirit of forgiveness, we need a spirit of usefulness. The more I grow in patience, forgiveness, meekness, gentleness, virtue, and faith, the more I realize I'm not just some nut out on the side of the road. I am something because I am God's creation. If the trees can wave their limbs and praise God, then how much more can we, with a mind and a brain, do for God? How much can we be used of Him? We don't recognize our usefulness until we draw closer to God.

Sometimes folks get saved, sanctified, and filled with the Holy Ghost, then immediately say, "Pastor, I feel a call on my life." Do not misunderstand. I love it when God works in people's lives. But I have a problem when those same folks won't take the time to grow in faith, patience, meekness, gentleness, or a spirit of forgiveness. They skip those attributes and want to go right to usefulness. There was a time when I wanted to be useful, but I caused several pastors great misery because I didn't know what I was talking about. I needed to grow in faith and gentleness. I needed a spirit of forgiveness rather than a judgmental attitude.

James 1:22 says, "Be ye doers of the word, and not hearers only, deceiving your own selves." In other words, don't pretend to be some sanctimonious spiritual giant. "I want to go to heaven, but I am not going to lift a finger to help anyone in this life.

Because I'm so spiritual, I don't have to mow the lawn. I don't have to pick up that piece of paper, and I sure don't have to go down and dig ditches." That's a sanctimonious illness. Jesus, even though He was God's own Son, paid the ultimate price. Don't you think He worked? He walked everywhere He went. Don't you think it was work to keep the faith while they beat and cursed and spit on Him? He lost the best of friends when Judas betrayed Him. He had to do more than just hear the Word; He had to be a doer of the Word.

In 2 Timothy 1:6 Paul said to Timothy, "Wherefore I put thee in remembrance that thou stir up the gift of God, which is in thee." He said to stir up the gift. If God gave you the ability to do landscaping, then commit to doing landscaping. If God gave you the ability to paint a wall, then tell your church, "I'm going to paint the wall." If God gave you the ability to be an usher, an altar worker, or a singer, then get up and do more than just hear the Word. There has been enough gospel preached into our spirits to save the whole world. But the reason we're not saving the whole world is we want, want, want. Give me, give me, give me; give me more, give me more.

There has to be a spirit of usefulness. Maybe you can't do anything physically for God, but you can give financially. A group of seniors meets in our church every Monday morning. They can't dig ditches or paint walls, but they come to the house of God and pray. That's a worthwhile ministry.

When you have all these attributes of grace working, you're going to recognize there is a fire inside you and that you need to do something about it. Even if you can't do anything else, you can praise and worship Him. You can lift your voice to the rooftop and let people know there is someone worth serving in this life—and that someone is Jesus Christ our Lord and Savior.

Inward Change/Outward Evidence

Things happen when grace takes place. When something happens inside, something happens on the outside too. Isaiah 61:10 says:

> I will greatly rejoice in the Lord, my soul shall be joyful in my God; for he hath clothed me with the garments of salvation, he hath covered me with the robe of righteousness, as a bridegroom decketh himself with ornaments, and as a bride adorneth herself with her jewels.

There are two kinds of dress that need to be understood here. One is the natural dress, and the other is spiritual dress. The natural dress deals with outward appearance. Our character and self-image are reflected by our apparel and mode of dress. Romans 12:2 says, "Be not conformed to this world: but be ye transformed by the renewing of your mind, that ye may prove what is that good, and acceptable, and perfect, will of God." And 1 Thessalonians 5:22 reminds Christians to "abstain from all appearance of evil."

We should do all we can to look presentable on behalf of Christ. Many people don't want to hear that. They would rather show up at church in shorts and flip-flops. But the more God gets inside me, the better I want to look for Him. It has to do with perception. If you dress like a fireman, you will be perceived as a fireman. If you dress as a policeman, you will be perceived as a policeman.

My granddaddy was a farmer. If you saw him in dress clothes, he just didn't look right. He had to have on those overalls. Granddaddy was a farmer, and he was received as a farmer and respected as a farmer. If you dress like a bum, you are going to be received as a bum. If you dress like an usher, you are going to be received as an usher. Please don't misunderstand. When you go out to work in the dirt, don't wear a suit. But when you are going to do something for God, let's look the best we can. We need to set a precedent that God is alive; He is for real and doing something spectacular in our lives.

The Bible tells us to do the very best we can. God's people are a blessed people, so we ought to act like we are blessed. If we act like a bunch of jerks, we are going to be received as jerks. If we act as if we are God-fearing people expecting a miracle, somebody is going to come in because they know a miracle is about to happen. Whether your vehicle is a 1927 or a 1997 model, you can make it presentable. Even if I'm poor as a house cat, I can put a smile on my face and dress my best. I'm also going to behave as good as I possibly can. Why? Because somebody out there needs hope and a life lift. I might be that life lift. Outward appearances do not tell about a person's spiritual status. But they do determine how one is perceived or accepted.

Then there is the inward dress. According to the biblical ideal, modesty is an inner spiritual grace that recoils from anything seemingly impure; it is chaste in thought and conduct and is free of crudeness and indecency in dress and behavior.

Ephesians 4:25 says, "Wherefore putting away lying, speak every man truth with his neighbor: for we are members one of another." There is death and life in the power of the tongue. When God dresses you up with patience and faith and a spirit of forgiveness, you are going to have to start talking differently. There is no sense in us wallowing in the hog pen. Let's get out on the mountaintop and say, "Look what Jesus did for me! He saved me from the life of sin. The Holy Ghost came and filled me with His power and His anointing and has given me wisdom where I was so ignorant before! He has helped me be something different than I have ever been!" Ephesians 4:31 tells us, "Let all bitterness, and wrath, and anger, and clamor, and evil speaking, be put away from you, with all malice."

Make Your Choice

Lots of folks have fooled themselves into believing they can have God and the world, but they can't. The Bible commands us to choose this day whom we are going to serve. You are going to have to make up your mind. You are either a child of God or you are not. You are either playing games or you are for real. Ephesians 5:1 says, "Be ye therefore followers of God, as dear children; and walk in love, as Christ also hath loved us, and hath given himself for us an offering and a sacrifice to God for a sweetsmelling savour." We are to follow God as children. I followed my mom and daddy for a few years and learned from them. We are learning to walk and love as Christ loved us. Verse 3 continues, "But fornication, and all uncleanness, or covetousness, let it not be once named among you, as becometh saints." When your name comes up in conversation, what do people say about you? Don't let this junk be named among you, the Word says, not once.

Verse 4 says, "Neither filthiness, nor foolish talking, nor jesting, which are not convenient: but rather giving of thanks." Read that again. But rather giving thanks. "For this ye know, that no whoremonger, nor unclean person, nor covetous man, who is an idolater, hath any inheritance in the kingdom of Christ and of God" (v. 5). Did you catch that? We can call ourselves spiritual all we want. But if we act like a bunch of idolaters, have ugly conversations, and don't represent the workmanship of Christ, the Bible says we don't have a part in heaven. We are just fooling ourselves. Let's not fool ourselves. Let's let Him clothe us with His righteousness.

The last part of Isaiah 61:10 says, "He hath clothed me with the garments of salvation." Even if friends die, health fails, and hopes are dashed, the Word says to rejoice in the Lord because He hath clothed you with an everlasting garment. We are the hope and peace of the world. When we should be down-and-out and frustrated, we need to show a sense of hope. We have to clothe our inner man with Christ Himself. We may be walking through the valley of the shadow of death, but we have hope. He has saved us and clothed us with the garments of salvation.

We need to take the natural dress and do the best we can with what we see and then take the internal dress and read, study, and listen to God's Word. The more you exercise God's Word of faith, meekness, and gentleness, and the more those things attach themselves to your life, the more the decay of wrongful doing has to go. The more God there is, the less evil there is.

A sad Christian sends mixed signals. When we say we're saved and are part of a vital ministry, but we always frown and complain, we send mixed signals. We can't live like that. We have to live as though we know everything is under control. And we can't do that unless we really believe it.

Radiance Shines

When these elements of grace are working in your life, they produce a radiant life. Have you ever noticed how the face of an expectant mother just glows? I don't want you to stare down expectant mothers, but if you pay attention, you will see that they glow because something's happening. This is the way it is with a believer. You have a radiance. Someone said to me recently, "I can see that everything is going well with you." When I asked how he knew, he said, "Because there is a glow."

When God gets more and more in you and produces that radiance, that kind of light, it's like being impregnated with a baby. It's like saying, "There is a baby inside me, and I'm growing in faith and patience. I'm growing in that spirit of forgiveness. God's doing something in me, and I'm about to give birth to a word that will change somebody's life." When we get into God, it produces a radiant life. If any many be in Christ, he is a new creature. He's not an old grump. He's not what he's always been. He is something different. I love it when folks who knew me years ago look at me now and say, "I don't see the same person. I see someone different."

Here's how the radiant life works. First of all, your life must be lived under the influence of faith. You must get under faith. This will not work without faith. Get in the Word and let it speak to you. Let the influence of faith work. Secondly, the radiant life comes from a love of God. The more you know His Word, the Bible, the more love you gain for God. It is the same in marriage. The more you get to know your spouse and your spouse gets to know you, the more love you have for one another. That's how two become one. Christ was married to the Church so we could be one. It's Christ and the Church together.

We need a radiant life because if we are not warming the world, then the world is chilling us. No matter what you've gone through, let this grace take hold and let that radiance go. Understand that there is a baby in there. God has planted something in your heart, and I can't wait to see what it's going to look like.

Faith and virtue, gentleness, patience, and a spirit of forgiveness are working in my life. They are bringing me closer to Christ and farther away from the world. And it's producing a radiance. Do you want that radiant life? Maybe you have tried and tried and tried, but you feel like you keep failing. May I say this to you? That's what grace is all about. Every time you fall, you don't fall as far down as you did the last time. Every time you get up, it is symbolic of taking another step. People ask why God in His infinite wisdom and power doesn't pick us up and keep us up. Because if we never fall, we will never completely understand His grace. And if we don't understand His grace, we can't have a radiant life. I want to see believers with the peace of God in their lives—people growing in grace regardless of their circumstances. Whatever we face, we can shine. If we ask Him, He will work in us to produce a radiant life.

Do You Want a Personal Relationship with Jesus Christ?

He wants one with you. He loves you so much that He came to this earth to bridge the gap between you and God. From the beginning of time, people have been separated from God because of the sins—or wrongs—they have committed. The Bible says, "As it is written, there is none righteous, no, not one. For all have sinned, and come short of the glory of God" (Romans 3:10, 23). Sin bears a penalty, and that penalty is death. "For the wages of sin is death, but the gift of God is eternal life through Jesus Christ our Lord" (Rom. 6:23).

God sent His Son to this earth to die on a cross as the payment for your sins and mine. Romans 5:8 tells us, "But God commended his love toward us, in that, while we were yet sinners, Christ died for us."

Christ's death on the cross is God's gift to you—if you accept it. How do we become part of God's family? By repenting, or turning from, our sins and asking God's forgiveness. Romans 10:9–11 says: "That if thou shalt confess with thy mouth the Lord Jesus, and shalt believe in thine heart that God hath raised him from the dead, thou shalt be saved. For with the heart man believeth unto righteousness; and with the mouth confession is made unto salvation. For the scripture saith, Whosoever believeth on him shall not be ashamed."

God's gift is available to everyone. "For whosoever shall call upon the name of the Lord shall be saved" (Rom. 10:13).

If you want to begin a new life in Christ, ask Him to forgive your sins and come into your heart. Thank Him for His gift to you of eternal life and ask Him to help you live each day for Him. Begin reading the Bible every day and get involved in a local church.

Bibliography/ Sources Used

Nelson's New Illustrated Bible Dictionary, Copyright © 1995, 1996, Thomas Nelson Publishers.

The Biblical Illustrator, by Joseph S. Exell, Copyright © 1973, Baker Book House, Grand Rapids, Michigan.

The NIV Matthew Henry Commentary In One Volume, Copyright © 1992, Zondervan Publishing House, Grand Rapids, Michigan.

Holman Bible Dictionary, Copyright © 1991, Holman Bible Publishers, Nashville, Tennessee.

The Thompson Chain Reference Bible, Copyright © 1988, B.B. Kirkbride Bible Company, Inc., Indianapolis, Indiana.

To order additional copies of

Salvation: It's Not What I Thought It Was

send $11.95 plus $3.95 shipping and handling to

Books Etc.
PO Box 4888
Seattle, WA 98104

or have your credit card ready and call

(800) 917-BOOK

or contact

Pastor Don R. Vining
15004 South Hwy 441
Summerfield, FL 34491
352-347-CARE (2273)